Horticulture in the North

A Guide to Fruit Growing in the Prairie Provinces of Canada.

With Chapters on the Selection and Cultivation of the Ornamental Trees and Plants Best Adapted to this Region, Handling and Care of Nursery Stock, the Home Garden, Beautifying the Home, Budding and Grafting, Plant Diseases and Insects, etc.

BY

D. W. BUCHANAN

Director The Buchanan Nursery Co., Past President The Western Horticultural Society.

St. Charles, Manitoba, 1907.

Entered according to the Act of the Parliament of Canada, in the year
One Thousand Nine Hundred and Seven, by D. W. Buchanan
at the Department of Agriculture,

INTRODUCTORY.

It is not the object of the writer to make this a pretentious work of Horticulture, but rather to be as brief and concise as possible, giving such information in condensed form as will meet the requirements of our people. About the only writings upon fruit growing in the prairie provinces of Canada are contained in the reports of horticultural societies. While some of the papers published by the horticultural societies are very valuable, they are naturally more or less scattered, incomplete and disjointed, and besides are not readily available to every one. Of all the standard works on Horticulture there is not one which will meet the conditions which here prevail. These books on Horticulture are only of value in a general way. What I will try to give is information adapted to this country. I am frequently in receipt of letters of inquiry on horticultural questions. It is just such questions as I am most frequently asked that I will try to answer here.

D. W. BUCHANAN.

St. Charles, Man., Jan., 1907.

NOTE—The chapter on "Handling and Planting Trees" should be read in connection with the chapters on the different kinds of fruit.

CONTENTS

CHAPTER I. Pages 9 to 14
CURRANTS.

General notes. A healthful fruit. Planting and cultivating. Time to plant. Plants last 30 years. Cultivate with a horse. Pruning. Time to prune. Grow in bush form—not on single stems. Mulching. Not a substitute for cultivation. Protection. Not usually needed. Injurious insects. The currant worm. Currant borer. Plant lice. Leaf hopper. Remedies. Diseases of the Currant. Prevention better than a cure. How to prevent. Remedies. Species and varieties. Origin of the Currants. The different species. Description of varieties

CHAPTER II. Pages 14 to 15
GOOSEBERRIES.

Related to the currant. Planting. Pruning. Protection. How applied. A profitable crop. Mildew. How to treat. How to prevent. Species and varieties. Origin of our gooseberries. Description of varieties adapted to planting in the prairie provinces.

CHAPTER III. Pages 15 to 20
STRAWBERRIES.

Faulty systems of cultivation. Some large plantations. Location of the strawberry plot. Preparation of soil. Time to plant. Methods of planting. Matted row system. Pinch off the blossoms. Hill system. How to handle the plants. Use only young plants. How to revive plants that have suffered from long shipment. How to plant. Winter protection. Don't use weedy cover. Time to cover. A new plan of growing the strawberry, which provides winter cover, protection against spring frost and early drouth. Spring frosts and drouth, the two great hindrances to strawberry growing, successfully overcome. Care of old beds. Mow and burn tops. Troublesome insects. Diseases. Remedies. Origin of our strawberries. Staminate and imperfect varieties. How complete failure of fruit may result. Description of varieties.

CHAPTER IV. Pages 20 to 26
RASPBERRIES.

Classification of varieties. Suckering varieties. Tip-rooting varieties. How propagated. A peculiar way of reproduction. Biennial and

CONTENTS.

perennial. Origin of varieties. The first parent of many choice varieties a native of our woods. How new varieties are produced. Location of the raspberry plot. Preparation of soil. Keep the soil cool and moist. Planting. Time to plant. Distance to plant. Close planting system. Cultivation. Mulching. Pruning. Hoeing off suckers. Cutting out old canes. Pinching back. Shortening the canes in the fall. Protection required. Mode of laying down and covering canes. Diseases. The best preventative. Some varieties not subject to disease. Anthracnose. Curle leaf. Orange rust. Remedies. Troublesome insects and the remedy. Description of varieties, red, yellow, purple and black.

CHAPTER V. Page 26

BLACKBERRIES.

Inquiries answered. Late ripening. Upright varieties. Recumbent varieties. Dewberries. How propagated. Origin. The best varieties.

CHAPTER VI. Page 27

THE BUFFALO BERRY.

Description of plant and fruit. An abundant fruiter. Why it sometimes fails to fruit. As an ornamental and hedge plant.

CHAPTFR VII. Page 27

RUSSIAN MULBERRY.

CHAPTER VIII. Pages 27 to 28

THE CRANBERRY.

Description. Not a garden plant. Could be grown in certain localities. Several species are native to Manitoba.

CHAPTER IX. Pages 28 to 30

THE GRAPE.

The wild grape of Manitoba. Description. Improving the native species. A desirable ornamental vine. How to breed new varieties. Propagation by cuttings. Origin of hardiest varieties. Cultivating, training and pruning. Winter protection. Hardiest varieties.

CONTENTS.

CHAPTER X. Pages 30 to 43

THE APPLE.

Reaches greatest state of perfection in the north. Planting in the prairie provinces. Errors of early planters. Worthless nursery stock. Unsuitable varieties. Results of apple growing in Minnesota. New varieties for our provinces. How to originate them. Experience gained in other climates of no value here. On the road to success. Not necessary to repeat early mistakes. How to produce a new race of hardy trees. The apples of the future. First rules to observe in planting apples. How the planter may grow his own trees. Top-grafting on hardy trees. Any one can do it. Pyrus baccata for top grafting. The weak points of a tree. Shelter for the apple. Trees planted in or near woods. Trees freeze dry. Location of apple orchard. Drainage and elevation. The worst location for apples. Soil. Too rich land forces a tender growth. Selecting trees. Planting large trees. Right age to plant. Hardy roots necessary. How trees are grown in the nurseries. Budding and grafting. Why budded apples are not desirable. Why most grafted trees have tender roots. How to avoid root-killing. Nearly all nursery trees have tender roots. The name of the variety no guide to the hardiness of the tree. May be grafted on a tender root. Planting the apple. Time to plant. How to plant. Distance to plant. Pruning. Best time to prune. Growing in bush form. Low trained trees. Long bare trunks bad. Water sprouts. How they grow. How to repair split crotches with little or no injury to the tree. Protecting the trunks from sunscald, mice and rabbits. Tree protectors. How to save a tree that has been barked by mice. Cultivation of the apple. Preserving soil moisture. The dust mulch. Cover crops. Mulching for fall. Diseases of the apple. Twig blight. Sunscald. Insects. The apple borer. Remedies. Origin and history of our apples and crabs. How to tell an apple from a crab tree at any time of year. Russian apples. Names badly mixed. Lists of hardy apples recommended for different sections. Hybrid apples. Names of varieties of apples that have been grown in Manitoba. Description of the hardiest apples and crabs.

CHAPTER XI. Pages 43 to 46

THE PLUM.

The Manitoba wild plum. Origin of the cultivated plums. Many distinct American species. **Prunus Americana. Prunus nigra.** How these have been improved. How to grow for our climate. Why trees brought in from the United States root kill. How this can be avoided. Why fruit does not set when trees blossom well. Best way to plant and cultivate the plum. Insects and the remedy. Diseases of the plum. Remedy for plum pocket, black knot, shot hole fungus. Varieties for this country.

CONTENTS. 7

CHAPTER XII. Pages 46 to 47

CHERRIES.

Cherries grown in Manitoba. Cherries in Minnesota and the Dakotas. Russian cherries. Our native cherries. How to improve and breed new varieties. The bush or sand cherry likely to prove a valuable species.

CHAPTER XIII. Pages 47 to 49

OUR NATIVE FRUITS.

Cultivated fruits originated from wild species. Some of our wild fruits superior to species from which some of the finest cultivated fruits now grown were originated. Breeding new varieties from our wild fruits. The native plum, grape, cranberry, buffalo-berry, sand or bush cherry, strawberries. Four native varieties of raspberries. Gooseberries, two native varieties. Currants. The juneberry. Viburnum, or high bush cranberry. Blueberries.

CHAPTER XIV. Pages 49 to 52

PROPAGATING FRUITS FROM SEED.

Cross-fertilizing. Hibridization. Systematic cross fertilizing. Not difficult to perform. How it is done. How to develop our truit interest and produce new and hardier varieties. How to grow strawberries, raspberries, currants, gooseberries, apples, plums, cherries, grapes, etc., from seed. Handling, storing, planting, cultivating and transplanting seedlings. Protecting seedlings from insects and from winter. "Damping off." How to water plants and seed beds. Watering badly done worse than not watering at all. Storing seedlings over winter. Why some seed remains two years in the ground before growing.

CHAPTER XV. Pages 52 to 56

GRAFTING AND BUDDING.

Various modes of propagating plants. Many different ways of grafting. Root grafting. Crown grafting. Stem grafting. Top grafting. Cleft grafting. Whip grafting. Time to graft. Storing the scions. Grafting wax. How made. Shield budding described. Care of budded trees. Top working by budding.

8 CONTENTS.

CHAPTER XVI. Pages 56 to 62

HANDLING AND PLANTING NURSERY STOCK.

Reviving stock dried out in shipment. Keeping stock till ready to plant. Mudding roots. Handling and planting evergreens. How to prepare trees for planting. Trimming roots. Cutting back tops. To handle frozen trees without damage. General principles of planting all kinds of trees and plants. Trees dormant for one year after planting. Cultivation better than mulching. A fallacy exposed. When to prune. How to prune. Pruning different species. Spring or fall planting. Heeling in trees. Advantages of purchasing stock in the fall. How to store stock over winter. Selecting nursery stock. Fibrous roots best. Small trees outgrow large ones. The reason explained.

CHAPTER XVII. Pages 62 to 67

THE HOME GARDEN AND SURROUNDINGS.

Beautifying the rural home. Improves the value of property. Promotes refined tastes. Minimizing hand labor. How to lay out the lawn. The vegetable and fruit garden. How to lay out. Health and happiness secured. The windbreak. An economy which no good farmer can afford to be without. How to lay out. Necessary to grow fruits. Preparing the soil and planting the windbreak. Varieties of trees to plant. Trees adapted to different soils.

CHAPTER XVIII. Pages 67 to 70

PLANT DISEASES. INJURIOUS INSECTS. SPRAYING MIXTURES.

Nature of fungi. Good cultivation the best preventative of disease. Potato blight. Leaf-eating insects. Sucking insects. How to prepare and use the various remedies for fungi and injurious insects.

CHAPTER XIX. Pages 70 to 72

TREES, SHRUBS AND PLANTS RECOMMENDED FOR THE PRAIRIE PROVINCES.

Trees for shelter belts and forest plantations. Evergreen trees. Ornamental trees and shrubs. Vines and climbers. Semi-hardy shrubs. Shrubs for hedges. Perennial flowers.

Horticulture in the North

CHAPTER I.

CURRANTS.

The currant is the best known and most largely grown of our small fruits. It is adapted to a wide variety of soils and a considerable variation in climate. While largely grown the currant is frequently shamefully neglected as regards attention and cultivation. The bushes are frequently planted along a fence where they receive no cultivation and remain for years until the grass sod around them becomes as tough as the native prairie. Worms are allowed to devour the foliage, thus injuring the crop of the following year. Pruning is quite neglected. That the currant will produce fruit at all under such circumstances, is a wonder. While often so neglected, there is no fruit that will respond to generous treatment more readily than the currant, by an increased yield of finer fruit. If the fruit is worth growing at all, it should be given reasonably good cultivation. If the reader has a lot of old bushes which have been so neglected, do not start in to try and improve them. It will be much more profitable to obtain new plants. The old, neglected bushes would not likely ever make good plants. Two year plants are the best for the beginner to start with.

Currants are said to be a very healthful fruit. We knew of one man who claimed to have been cured of indigestion by a liberal use of red currants. Used in the form of that rural delicacy known as green currant pie, we would not regard them as very healthful, but we can quite believe much that is said in favor of currants from a health point of view, when fresh, fully ripe fruit is used. The sweeter varieties of currants, such as White Grape, when fully ripe, are certainly both delicious and healthful, when eaten fresh, with sugar and cream. The juice of any of the currants makes a delightful drink, which should be extremely healthful. The thrifty housewife will understand how to preserve either the whole fruit or the juice for use at any season of the year. For jelly, or for marketing, the fruit should be gathered before it is too ripe, that is, while some of the berries on the ends of the bunches are still somewhat green. For home canning or table use ripe fruit is best.

PLANTING AND CULTIVATION—As already stated, the currant will grow in almost any kind of land, but rich, well drained land is desirable for best results. If a heavy crop of fine fruit is wanted, rich soil and abundant cultivation should be given. Starting with two year old plants, they should be (See chapter on "Handling and Planting Nursery Stock") planted in rows, five to six feet apart each way. They are sometimes planted closer, but we prefer the longer distance. Do not plant along a walk or fence, but in the open garden, where the ground can be given horse cultivation at least one way between the rows. If planted on a large scale they should be so arranged that horse cultivation can be given between the rows both ways. See chapter on "The Home Garden and Surroundings" for further information regarding the planting and cultivation of currants and other fruits. The land should be prepared for this or any other fruits by thorough cultivation and deep plowing. Land that is in good shape for ordinary garden crops should do. Planting should be done either early in the spring or in the fall. If in the fall, we prefer rather early fall, so the plants will become somewhat established before winter. If the weather is unseasonably warm, or the ground very dry, it would be better to wait for more favorable conditions. We have planted currants in the fall even after the ground had begun to freeze with good results, but if the ground is in good condition, toward the close of September or early October is a better time. The same rules should be observed in fall planting as in spring planting, except that in the fall plants should be well banked up and small plants like currants may be entirely covered. Once planted, the main thing is cultivation, which should be done with a one-horse cultivator between the rows, not once or twice during the growing season, but frequently. This cultivation should be kept up each and every year as long as the plants are desired to produce fruit. A currant plantation, well treated, will give good results for many years. In the East twenty to thirty years is allowed for the currant. Cultivation should be started early in the spring, early cultivation being the most effective. A light plow may sometimes be used to advantage for the first cultivation in the spring. Towards picking season cultivation may be suspended to avoid injury or shaking off of the fruit, but at least one or two good cultivations should be given, starting soon after the fruit is gathered. This will assist the plants to retain foliage and improve the fruit prospect for the next year.

PRUNING—In our severe climate there is sometimes a tendency to overdo the pruning of trees and plants, especially on the part of those who come from a moister and milder climate. The currant, however, will be improved by considerable pruning, which, like all other pruning, should be done systematically and with a definite object in view. Toward the close of the growing season, or early in the spring is the best time to prune. Many varieties of currants send up a number of new shoots each year. The pruning should consist in removing all but three or four of the strongest of these new shoots each year. At the same time some of the oldest branches should be cut out close to the ground. By following this plan the bush will be entirely renewed every few years, always remembering that three or four year old wood usually will produce the most fruit. The plants should, therefore, be a few years old

CURRANTS.

before the old wood is cut out, unless, of course, some of the old wood should be damaged by disease, insects, or from some other cause, in which case it would usually be better removed.

These directions as to pruning are based on the theory that the plants are growing on the bush plan. Sometimes currants are grown on a single stem, like a small tree. This plan is entirely unsuited to this country. Our heavy winds may break off the single stem, and the plant is gone. When grown in bush form, the snow is retained about the roots much better during winter, which gives protection to the roots, and also assists in retaining moisture in spring and summer. The work of the currant borer is alone a sufficient reason against growing on the single stem plan. The stem is often so damaged by these insects as to destroy the branch entirely. If the currant is on a single stem, the entire plant is lost, while if there are several stems, only one may be lost.

MULCHING—This question of mulching is one upon which we have been asked a great many questions. Many people seem to think that they can keep weeds down and save cultivation by mulching. The mulch has its place and is sometimes useful and beneficial, but as a substitute for cultivation, or for keeping down weeds, we regard it as very unsatisfactory. Strong weeds will push through almost any thickness of mulch that it would be safe to use. Cultivation, without the mulch, in our climate, is far better than a mulch without cultivation. Frequent surface cultivation provides a dust or soil mulch, the loose surface soil acting as a mulch for the soil underneath. The soil is more easily cultivated than when covered with litter, and there is less tendency to grow weeds. Manure may be scattered about between the rows, preferably in the fall, and worked into the soil in the spring, with good results for the crop. Wood ashes is also valuable.

PROTECTION—The hardy varieties of currants will not require much in the way of winter protection. In severe or exposed locations, the best protection would be a covering of brush, to gather and hold the snow. If the brush is cut in the summer it will retain the leaves and in this form makes a more desirable cover.

INSECTS—The insect most frequently found upon the currant is the common currant worm. The mature insect, in the form of a fly, not unlike the house fly, lays her eggs on the under side of the leaf, in the spring. The young worms, soon after hatching, at once attack the foliage and where numerous soon strip the bushes. They are about three quarters of an inch long when fully grown and of a greenish yellow color. A second brood sometimes appears late in the summer. The currant worm is very easily destroyed. Powdered hellebore may be applied either in a dry form, mixed with flour, about equal parts of each, or in water, one ounce to the pailful. Early in the season spraying with Paris Green of ordinary strength (See chapter on Plant Diseases, Insects and Spraying) may be resorted to, but that should not be used when the fruit is approaching the picking season. Hellebore is a less dangerous poison, but even with this, a little time should elapse, after application, before the fruit is used. A shower will usually remove this poison, which is less tenacious than Paris Green. If used dry, hellebore should be dusted on when the foliage is moist with dew. Under no circumstances should these insects be allowed to destroy the foliage, either before or after the crop is gathered. The plants cannot maintain a healthy growth and fruit well if they have lost their foliage. Remember the leaves are the lungs and stomach of a plant.

CURRANT BORER—More difficult to eradicate is the imported Currant Borer. This is a whitish worm or caterpillar which tunnells through the centre of the canes. The mature insect takes the form of a fly or moth, and lays her eggs on the stem. The larvae remain in the stem until the following season, when the fly or moth is developed. This suggests the remedy, which is, to cut out the infested canes in the fall or early spring and burn them, cutting close to the ground so as to be sure to get below the tunnel. The injured canes can readily be detected by their sickly appearance. Canes which have been tunnelled by the currant borer, are liable to break off.

PLANT LICE—The currant is frequently infested with lice or aphis, which may be found on the under side of the leaves. The infested leaves curl and assume a blistered appearance. These lice belong to the class known as suckering insects. They do not eat the foliage, but suck the juice from the leaves, and are, therefore, injurious to the plants, though the damage done is not as apparent as in the case of the leaf eaters. Another similar pest is the Leaf Hopper, a small, greenish insect. These sucking insects are best treated by spraying with coal oil emulsion. (See chapter on Plant Diseases and Spraying.) This spray kills by contact, and it is necessary to reach the under side of the leaf, which requires a sprayer of considerable force.

DISEASES—In common with practically all other forms of vegetable life, the currant is subject to attack from fungi in various forms. An early casting of the foliage may generally be attributed to leaf rust. The treatment for all forms of fungi is much the same, and is dealt with in the chapter on Plant Diseases and Spraying. Good results cannot be expected from plants which suffer from rust, smut, mildew, etc., and every effort should be made to prevent and destroy these diseases. Early treatment is by all means the most effective. One treatment in good time is worth several later on. The rule that prevention is better than a cure applies with double force in the case of plant fungi. Good cultivation is the best preventative against plant disease.

SPECIES AND VARIETIES—All our well known varieties of red and white currants belong to the one species **(Ribes rubrum)** which is a native of Northern Europe and Asia. **Ribes negrum,** the black currant, is also a native of the same regions. To that species most of our well known black currants belong. A few varieties of black currants belonging to the species **Ribes aureum** have been introduced during recent years, but they are not very generally known yet. To the latter

CURRANTS.

species belongs the variety known as Crandall. The fruit of varieties belonging to this species is large and glossy black, flowers yellow and sweet scented. Forms of this species are grown for ornamental purposes. They are quite distinct from our well known black currants in foliage, flower and fruit. **Ribes aureum** is a native of the Mississippi valley and westward. The native black currant of Manitoba belongs to the species **Ribes Americanum**, while our native red currant is closely related to the red currant of Europe, which has furnished us with so many excellent garden varieties. There are many varieties of currants, but the medium to small varieties, in reds, are usually the most abundant fruiters. Those producing very large fruit are as a rule not as prolific. Only a few of the best will be described.

WHITE GRAPE—This is the sweetest of all the currants. Exceedingly hardy and prolific. For home use very desirable. For market red currants usually sell better. Upright grower.

FAY'S PROLIFIC—A variety which has been liberally advertised and extensively planted. Fruit very large, red. Bush spreading habit. A weak grower in our climate and not always hardy.

RED DUTCH—About the hardiest variety and very productive. Fruit medium to small. Hangs well to bushes. Plant a strong, upright grower. A good sort for general planting.

VICTORIA—Fruit red, large, hangs well to bushes; prolific. Valuable for home use or market. A late variety.

LA VERSAILLES AND CHERRY—These two varieties which closely resemble each other, are very large fruited sorts, but, like Fay's, not as hardy as the other varieties mentioned.

NORTH STAR—Red, medium sized fruit. A variety which is regarded with favor in Minnesota, where it originated. Requires very rich soil and good cultivation.

RABY CASTLE—Medium sized fruit, red. Bush somewhat spreading habit. This variety is regarded with favor by some of our best fruit growers.

STEWART—A very strong growing, upright variety; hardy. Perhaps the hardiest of the large fruiting red sorts. Thick, healthy foliage, which remains longer on the bushes than is the case with perhaps any other variety. Prolific. A desirable variety, but the dense foliage, while indicating health and vigor, is a disadvantage in picking the fruit.

POMONA—Fruit large, bright red, good quality. Very productive. Ripens very early. Plant hardy and healthy. A promising new variety.

RED CROSS—A new red variety which is recommended by the Minnesota Horticultural Society, but which is considered by some who have tried it as not hardy enough for severe locations.

LONG BUNCH HOLLAND—Fruit medium size, bright red, but of rather poor quality. Not prolific.

LONDON MARKET—Fruit medium to large, bright red, large clusters. A productive and reliable sort.

WILDER—A new variety which has received liberal advertising. Our tests with this variety have not proved satisfactory, and I am inclined to rate it as not hardy enough for general planting here.

BLACK CURRANTS—There are not as many varieties of black currants as of the reds, and several of the varieties which have been most generally planted are rather unproductive. Lee's Prolific is one of the best in point of productiveness. Black Naples and Black Champion are well known and hardy sorts, but not as prolific as the first named. The black currants compare favorably with red varieties in point of hardiness.

CHAPTER II.
GOOSEBERRIES.

It will not be necessary to devote much space to the gooseberry, as nearly the same treatment recommend for the currant will apply to this fruit. The gooseberry belongs to the same family as the currant, and is subject to attack from the same insects. It is more subject to mildew than the currant. Instructions for planting and pruning are practically the same as for the currant.

PROTECTION—In severe or exposed locations gooseberries will require more protection than is usually given to the currant. The best protection is a liberal covering with brush. Where there is plenty of snow an excellent cover will be formed by the banking of the snow in the brush. The plants are sometimes mounded up with earth, but it is troublesome to remove the earth in the spring. Many growers here have not succeeded well with gooseberries and have concluded that the plants are too tender for our climate. Others have done remarkably well, and have found them very profitable. Our own experience has been that the gooseberry is the most profitable crop we have grown. One year with another the plants have been exceedingly productive.

MILDEW—This disease is first noticeable on the foliage, in the form of a white mould. A closer inspection will sometimes show that the fruit is also affected or discolored by a brownish mould. The leaves dry and drop off and the new growth of wood is sometimes destroyed. Crowding the plants induces mildew. Plenty of room and good cultivation are the best preventatives. Wet, undrained soil is also productive of this trouble. Where mildew has been troublesome, spray early in the spring, even before the buds are fully opened, with flour of sulphur, about one ounce to the pail. Dissolve in hot water. This should be applied after every heavy rain. The early sprayings will prove much more effective than the later treatments, and should not be neglected on any account.

SPECIES AND VARIETIES—The only varieties of gooseberries which it is safe to plant freely in our prairie provinces belong to the species **Ribes hirtellum**. This species is a native of Canada and northern portions of the United States. The large European varieties are not suited to our climate.

HOUGHTON—This is decidedly the most satisfactory variety for this country. It is the hardiest and most prolific sort. The fruit is of good quality, small to medium size, and of a reddish shade when ripe. If reasonable care is given in cultivating, pruning, etc., the fruit will usually be of very fair size, but if neglected, small fruit will be the result.

SMITH'S IMPROVED—Oblong, green berries, larger than Houghton. Moderately productive. Good quality.

DOWNING—Larger fruit than the two varieties preceding, and not as tart flavor. Pale green color. Better for eating raw but not as good for preserving. Not as hardy as the preceding varieties.

PEARL—Resembles the last named variety, in size, color, and appearance of fruit. Fairly hardy.

CHAPTER III.

STRAWBERRIES.

Perhaps less success has attended the attempts at growing strawberries in Manitoba and other parts of our prairie country than has been the experience with the fruits already considered in these pages. This, however, does not prove that strawberries cannot be grown to fair advantage here, but rather, that the mode of cultivation best adapted to this country was not known to the planter. The writer has given much attention to this fruit and has worked out a system of cultivation which has proved quite successful. Others have been quite successful in growing strawberries in Manitoba, even on quite a large commercial scale, and have been able to ship in considerable quantities to the Winnipeg market. When the best plan of growing strawberries is understood, this delicious fruit will no doubt be much more extensively grown.

LOCATION AND PREPARATION OF SOIL—More care is necessary in selecting a location and preparing the soil for strawberries than for most other fruits. It is absolutely necessary that the plants should be sheltered from the wind. Planting the strawberry rows between rows of raspberries or some bush fruits, affords some protection, but in addition to this a good wind break is desirable. It will be very difficult to secure a good setting of young plants in an exposed location. The soil for strawberries should be very carefully prepared. Many varieties do best on a loamy soil, but on the heavy land of the Red River valley the plants seem to thrive. The land should be plowed deeply the previous year, and it not very rich should be well manured. Only land in a high state of cultivation should be used, free from weeds and sod. Harrow the ground well in the spring and it will be ready for planting.

TIME, AND METHODS OF PLANTING—A great many inquiries come to us every season as to the best time to plant strawberries. I will answer these here, as I have so often done in private correspondence, by saying that spring is the only time to plant strawberries in this country. In our short season, the young plants are not sufficiently developed to permit of early fall planting, but even if good plants could be obtained, we would advise against planting in the fall. Late fall planting would be even more likely to lead to failure. In our climate, weather and soil conditions are seldom favorable for the fall planting of strawberries. Fairly early spring planting is desirable, but in case of dry ground in the early spring, planting should be deferred for a time.

MATTED ROWS—Strawberries are most frequently grown on what is known as the matted row system. Nearly all large growers follow this plan. The rows are marked out about four feet apart, and in these rows the plants are set from one foot to 18 inches apart. This is closer than is usually recommended, but is not too close for our climate, as the plants do not set as freely here as in moister climates where the season is longer. The lesser distance is safer. The space between the rows should be kept well cultivated at frequent intervals, for which the one-horse cultivator is used, always cultivating in the same direction after the runners start, so as not to drag the runners forward or backward by cultivating in opposite directions. Cultivation must be kept up until fall, or toward the end of August. In addition to the horse cultivation, it is advisable to go over the rows several times with a hand implement, and throw a little earth over the runners here and there, to hold them in place. If the runners are shifted about with the wind, the young plants will have a slim chance to take root. This work is very important in our dry and windy climate. Weeds growing between the plants, not reached by the cultivator, should be removed by hand. It is also necessary to go over the rows the first season and pinch off the blossom stems as soon as they are sufficiently developed. It is not fruit, but healthy, strong plants that are wanted the first year. The parent plants should not be allowed to exhaust themselves in producing fruit, but should give all their energy to producing new plants. It is these new plants that will give the fruit crop the following year. If the work has been a success, by the fall of the first season a solid row of plants, 18 inches wide, should completely cover the ground.

HILL SYSTEM—Strawberries are sometimes grown on the hill system. The plants are usually set somewhat closer together and all runners are kept hoed off as soon as they appear. In that way very large, individual plants are produced, and larger and finer fruit is secured, but in less quantity in proportion to the labor bestowed upon them. The hill system is only followed in small garden plantations. There are other systems which are more or less of a modification of the matted

STRAWBERRIES.

row plan, or, we might say, a compromise between the matted row and hill system. The principal followed in these modifications is to limit the number of runners allowed to each plant, curtail the number of new plants and keep the matted row within narrower limits. These modifications of the matted row system, of course, entail more labor. It is sometimes advised to cut off the first runners that start, on the theory that stronger runners will follow. In our climate, at any rate, this practice would be objectionable. It is advisable to have the young plants established as early as possible, owing to possibility of dry weather later, rather than to put them back by hoeing off the early runners.

HANDLING PLANTS—Strawberry plants require careful handling before planting. Plants should not be kept in a dark place, or packaged up any longer than can be avoided. If plants have been received from a distance, they should be unpacked at once, but should not be immediately exposed to strong light. Heel in or plant temporarily in a shaded location, until the plants have recovered a good color. They can be planted closely in a slight trench and watered easily. If plants are received when the ground is very dry, the same plan may be followed. Only young plants, that have never fruited, should be used for starting new beds.

PLANTING—Special care in planting should be followed by those who wish to succeed with strawberries. Broken or withered leaves should be picked off before planting. The blossom stem, if sufficiently developed, may also be pinched off, otherwise this will have to be done shortly after planting. It is also desirable to shorten up the roots. In planting the roots should be spread out and the soil well pressed around the roots. Care must be observed to plant just the right depth. See illustrations herewith. The one plant is set just the right depth, with roots well spread out. The other illustration shows the roots planted in a mat. Strawberries require more care in setting than most other plants, particularly as to the depth of planting. The crown must be just even with the surface. If planted too deep, so that the crown is covered, the plants will slowly die. If too shallow, the roots will dry out. The plants must not be exposed to sun or wind while the planting is being done. Keep them covered and moist. Select a cool, cloudy day for planting.

If the weather should turn very warm and bright, or windy, soon after planting, shading may be necessary for a time. This may be accomplished by scattering light straw or hay over the plants, or shading with boards.

PROTECTION IN WINTER—The best protection for the strawberry is a good covering of snow. We are not always sure of sufficient snow and some other cover will often be necessary. Brush, which has been cut in the summer and has the dry leaves attached, makes a fair cover. The brush will gather the snow and give good winter protection. In the spring, when the brush is removed, it will be found that the leaves have fallen from the branches and will remain as a mulch for the plants. Clean straw, free from seeds, or hay, cut late in the season after the seed has all fallen make good cover. If hay or straw with seed in it is used, the strawberry bed will be destroyed by a mass of weeds the following season. The cover should not be put on too early. Wait until the ground is frozen slightly. Mould is induced by early covering, if the weather should turn mild, and the plants may be destroyed.

My plan of covering strawberries is as follows: If the weather is likely to be very cold before snow comes, I cover with hay cut late in the fall, not too heavily. If a good fall of snow comes before the plants are covered, so much the better. This is the most favorable condition. Now cover heavily with light hay or straw, on top of the snow. One foot will not hurt the plants. A good cover on top of the snow will hold the plants back in the spring until all danger of spring frost is over. By this plan the ground will be kept cool and moist until the fruiting season is over. Thus the two great hindrances to successful strawberry growing in this climate, namely, spring frosts and early drouth, are overcome. Remove the mulch gradually or in cloudy weather and leave a considerable portion of it to cover the space well between the rows. The cover can be left on very late in the season, when put on on top of the snow, without injuring the plants. Watch the plants and remove when growth starts. If there should be indications of frost after the plants have started to bloom, the cover which has been left between the rows, may quickly be scattered over the plants. They will not take any harm if this cover should be left on for a day or two, should the weather continue cold. We have never found it necessary to cover plants to protect from spring frost when the cover was put on after a good fall of snow. In some seasons the cover was not put on until toward spring, before the snow began to melt, with excellent results. The only drawback to this system is the possibility of severe weather early in the winter before snow comes.

KEEPING BEDS IN BEARING—How long will the strawberry bed continue to produce good crops is often asked. We have had a fair crop the fourth year. On our soil the second crop is usually the best, and we think this will frequently hold good on other soils in this climate, as in our short season the plants often do not become very thick the first year. Three crops, as a rule, will be found the limit of profitable production.

Sometimes only two, after which the plants should be plowed up. If the beds are to be retained for another season, they should be mowed soon after the fruiting season is over, and the refuse raked off and burned. The width of the rows may be reduced by cutting off a furrow on either side and running the cultivator between the rows. This will give room for new plants to set. Weeds and old plants may be cut out with the hoe.

INSECTS—Insects have not been found very troublesome to strawberry plants in this country. Grub, of two or three kinds sometimes attacks the roots and cut off the plants so that they die. Usually troublesome only on soddy soil. No sure remedy.

DISEASES—Leaf blight or rust has sometimes proved troublesome. Beds badly rusted have been observed, but often a good crop of fruit is gathered before the rust becomes serious. Mow and burn the foliage as soon as the crop is gathered. Spray with Bordeaux mixture early in the spring, and also spray new beds. Avoid varieties subject to rust.

SPECIES AND VARIETIES—There are several species of strawberries, all natives of America, which have been improved by cultivation. From one of these species known as the Alpine or wood strawberry **(Fragaria vesca)** several varieties have been produced. They are known as everbearing varieties. They are not productive and are not generally known. Many of our readers will be familiar with the wild form of this species. Another species **(Fragaria grandiflora)** is a native of South America, and is cultivated to some extent. Nearly all our best known cultivated varieties belong to the species **Fragaria virginiana**. This is our well known common wild strawberry, from which an enormous number of named varieties have been produced.

It is a difficult matter to select a brief list of varieties to recommend for general planting. The number of varieties offered is so great as to be bewildering, many of them excellent sorts. Scores of new varieties are offered annually, and some of these are "boomed" energetically as something better than older sorts, and find buyers at fancy prices. It rarely happens, however, that these new varieties are better than a score or more of well known sorts. In purchasing strawberry plants, the buyer should know that there are two classes of plants, known respectively as staminate, or bi-sexual, and pistillate, or imperfect flowered sorts. The staminate plants have perfect flowers, the male and female organs being combined in the one blossom. Varieties having perfect blossoms will produce fruit when planted alone. The varieties which produce only imperfect or pistillate blossoms (that is, blossoms having the female organs only) must not be planted alone or complete failure will be the result. These pistillate varieties should be planted along with a staminate sort, to ensure fertilization. They may be planted alternately in the same row, or in alternate rows. Sometimes two or three rows of pistillate are planted to one of staminate. The best pistillate sorts are generally regarded as more productive than the staminate plants, hence the desirability of planting more of them, with only a sufficient number of staminate plants to ensure fertilization. Where only one variety is planted it should, of course, be a staminate sort. In nursery catalogues staminate varieties are usually distinguished by the letter S (staminate) placed after the name of the variety, while pistillate sorts are distinguished by the letter P or I (imperfect).

It is further well to remark that different varieties of strawberries succeed best on different soils. It is, therefore, advisable to try several varieties. About 100 to 200 plants would be sufficient for the home use of a small family, if good results were obtained from that number. We will only give a limited list of a few favorite varieties.

CRESCENT—Pistillate—A vigorous, healthy variety. Productive. Fruit fairly large, bright red, firm. Grown extensively as a market berry. Season early.

WARFIELD—An exceedingly productive pistillate sort. Healthy, strong grower. Fruit medium size, dark red, firm. A fine market variety. Season early.

HAVERLAND—Another very productive pistillate sort. Fruit better flavor than Warfield, but not as firm, and, therefore, not as desirable for marketing. Plants healthy. Season later than preceding.

BEDERWOOD—Perfect, strong, healthy plants. A variety that has been in favor for a considerable time, and used largely for planting with pistillate sorts.

SENATOR DUNLOP—Vigorous and healthy, perfect variety. Fruit medium to large, firm. Good quality. Mid season.

SHARPLESS—An old, perfect flowering variety. Not as largely grown as formerly, but one that seems well adapted to our soil and climate. Fruit very large, light red. Mid season. Other favorite varieties are: Enhance, S; Lovett, S; Splendid, S; Mary, S; Clyde, S; Sample, P; Gandy, S. The last is a good late variety.

CHAPTER IV.

RASPBERRIES.

Raspberries are usually spoken of as red, white, black, yellow or purple varieties. From a horticultural, or, at least, botanical point of view, this is not a proper way of considering the different species and varieties. Generally speaking, raspberries belong to two classes, namely, the suckering varieties and the tip varieties. The former are propagated by suckers which strike out very freely from the roots of most varieties belonging to this class. Most of the red and white or yellow varieties belong to this class. The raspberries known as tip varieties are natur ally increased in a somewhat peculiar manner. The young shoots at first take an upright position, but gradually as growth proceeds the canes assume a weeping or rainbow form. The canes continue to grow downward, until late in the summer the tips will be found resting on the ground. In this position they will root from the tip, if the conditions are favorable, and thus a new plant is formed. In our climate, often dry and windy in the late summer, the conditions are not favorable for tip rooting, and this will not take place in an exposed position unless the tips are covered with earth. The black varieties belong to the tip-rooting class. Some of the purple and yellow varieties are naturally increased both by suckers and from tip-rooting. Such varieties are supposed to be hybrids between the suckering and tip-rooting species.

All the raspberries are both biennial and perennial. The roots are perennial and send up new canes every year. The tops are biennial. The fruit is produced on the canes of the previous season's growth, and soon after the fruit is ripe the canes begin to die. By the next spring these canes will be quite dry and will generally snap off at the ground if bent downward. Thus the new canes of one year become the fruiting canes of the following season, after which their usefulness is gone and they are removed and burned.

The raspberry has a very wide range in its wild state. One or more species are found in almost every part of America that is at all adapted to husbandry. There are a great many named varieties of the suckering raspberries now offered by our nurserymen. These are usually red, but some are yellow or amber colored. These have originated from the common wild species, botanically known as **Rubus strigosus,** which is a native of our own provinces. The tip-rooting varieties have come from the species **Rubus occidentalis.** This is also a native American species, with a more restricted northerly range than **Rubus strigosus.** There is a great variation in the hardiness of the different varieties offered. Some varieties succeed very well in our western prairie provinces, when given reasonable protection, and a few varieties will sometimes produce fair crops of fruit without any cover, in favorable localities. New varieties of the raspberry, in common with practically all other fruits, are produced by growing plants from the seed. Propagating fruits from seed will be treated in a chapter by itself, which see.

LOCATION AND PREPARATION OF SOIL—The raspberry plantation should be sheltered from the warm, drying winds of summer. Hot, drying winds are very damaging to this crop, especially in the fruiting season. The fruiting season is sometimes greatly shortened by such weather, and sometimes the fruit is dried and shrivelled by very warm, windy weather. Protection from wind, especially on the south and the west, is, therefore, desirable. Keeping the soil cool and moist by cultivation or mulching greatly assists in tiding the crop over periods of unfavorable weather. The land for raspberries should be rich and in a high state of cultivation, and should be plowed deeply the fall before planting.

PLANTING—Raspberries are usually planted in the spring, though the suckering varieties may be planted in the fall. As growth starts very early in the spring, it is sometimes an advantage to plant in the fall, providing the weather is favorable. For fall planting the soil should contain sufficient moisture and be in the proper state of cultivation. If dry, it would be wise to defer planting until spring. Fall planting should be done fairly early, as recommended for currants. Late in the fall some earth could be thrown up toward the plants, and a good mulch covering the rows would be very beneficial, and ensure safe wintering. Black or tip-rooting kinds should not be planted in the fall. Raspberries should be planted in rows from six to eight feet apart, according to variety. The tip-rooting sorts require more room than most red varieties. Some varieties are much stronger growers than others, and consequently require more space. The strong growing sorts, especially in black varieties, are not as well adapted to our climate. They are much more difficult to cover for winter protection. Low growing varieties are more easily handled. If a considerable number of plants are to be set out, the most expeditious way is to plow furrows and plant at the desired intervals in the furrow. The tip rooting varieties will require more careful treatment in planting. Careless planting will result in the loss of many plants. Too deep planting is a fruitful source of loss in planting black raspberries. Plant only the same depths as the plants grew before moving, spread the roots carefully in their natural position and firm the soil around them. Suckering varieties may be planted a little deeper than they formerly grew, especially in light soil. The plants may be placed from two to six feet apart in the rows, according to variety.

CLOSE PLANTING—Good results have sometimes been obtained from a system of close planting. This system is applicable only to the suckering or upright varieties. It has been adopted for exposed locations. The plants are allowed to form a continuous row instead of being grown in hills, and the rows are only three or four feet apart. The object of this plan is to gather snow in winter to protect the plants. In some locations plantations laid out in this way will drift full of snow and almost completely cover the plants. The objection to this plan of growing the raspberry is that it is not favorable to that good cultivation which is necessary for the raspberry. We would not expect plants grown on this principle to endure in good form for as many years as when planted in the usual way.

CULTIVATION—Frequent cultivation with the one horse cultivator between the rows is very necessary for success in growing this fruit. A surface layer of loose earth to prevent evaporation of moisture will greatly help to overcome the danger from warm, dry, windy weather. Cultivation should be kept up vigorously, especially up to the time of maturing of the fruit. The first cultivation in the spring may be done with a light, one-horse plow. Keep the land level between the rows.

MULCHING—A heavy mulch between the rows is often very valuable. Where there is a liberal space between the rows, the mulch may be placed along the rows and the centre kept cultivated, or the mulch may cover the entire space. The mulch should be put on before very warm weather sets in. A green mulch is good. Where a wide space is allowed between the rows, a vegetable crop of some kind may be grown in the centre space. Especially in the case of a new plantation, the space between the rows may be utilized for some other crop, as no mulch is required the first year.

PRUNING—The suckering varieties will send up a great many shoots every year. Those not reached by the cultivator should be kept hoed out, leaving four to six strong canes to each plant, for fruiting the following year. Old canes that have fruited may be removed in the fall after fruiting, or the next spring. If the plants are to be covered for winter, get the old canes out of the way in the fall. If the plants are to be left standing over winter, the old canes may be left until spring to assist in gathering snow. In the case of a new plantation, it is not advisable to let more than two or three canes grow the first year, and in the case of a weak growth, it would be better to cut off all canes the first fall and not allow any fruiting the second year. The black and other tip-rooting varieties will not send up as many shoots as the red sorts, but the surplus canes should be removed in the same manner.

PINCHING BACK—Pinching back the raspberry is practiced in many sections where this fruit is grown extensively. The plan generally adopted is as follows: The young shoots that have been selected for fruiting the following year are pinched off when about 12 to 18 inches high. This will cause them to send out lateral branches. Both suckering and tip varieties are treated the same. The following spring the lateral branches of the tip-rooting kinds are cut back again, but the suckering kinds are not usually further pruned. While this system of pinching back the raspberry gives satisfactory results in fruit sections further south, a number of our best horticulturists here claim that they have not experienced any increase in the crop from pinching. If this system is followed it must be done early and the young shoots must not be over 18 inches high at the most. In some cases there will be no formation of lateral branches, especially if the pinching off is not done in good time. If not pinched back in the early summer, the canes may be shortened back when the work of covering is being done in the fall.

PROTECTION—Generally speaking, all varieties of raspberries require winter protection. Even in regions where the winter is much milder than here, it is customary with many growers to cover the canes in winter. The Turner and Philadelphia, red varieties, have sometimes produced fair crops of fruit without cover. These two varieties, hardy as they are, will sometimes fail without protection. To ensure a good crop of fruit, cover is necessary. The plan of protection followed is to bend the canes to the ground. This is done best with a two-tined fork, at the same time pressing with the foot at the base of the plant. Two men are necessary to perform the work expeditiously, one covering the canes as they are bent over, with sufficient earth to hold them down. In the case of strong plants, especially where they have been pinched back and have made a very stiff, stocky growth, it will be necessary to loosen the earth at the root with a digging fork, to allow of bending the plant from the root. This will reduce the danger of snapping the canes. Bending or laying down the canes should not be undertaken when they are frozen, as they are liable to be broken. The canes may be put down before frosty weather and the covering completed later on. The canes should be put down in a straight row, with the tops all in one direction. A furrow may then be turned with the plow toward the row on each side, and the work of covering completed with a hand tool. For the hardiest sorts simply laying the canes down and covering them with sufficient earth to keep them down will often prove sufficient protection to ensure a good crop of fruit. There is always, however, danger of severe weather with bare ground, and in such case a good cover of earth entirely over the canes will be found necessary for nearly all varieties. A mulch is sometimes added to the earth cover. In case of severe weather with little or no snow on the ground, many varieties will require the mulch, if only lightly covered with earth.

DISEASES—Good cultivation is the best safeguard against disease. In the case of plants that have fruited for a number of years—say six or seven years—it would, perhaps, be better to cut and burn the plants and plow them up should disease appear, and start again with fresh plants on new soil. Plants for a new plot, however, should not be taken from a diseased plantation. A change of variety is also sometimes advisable, where disease of any kind has gained a foothold. Some varieties will be found much less subject to disease than others. This is true of all fruits as well as raspberries. Plants showing any tendency to disease should be dug out and burned. Prompt treatment of this nature may check the spread of some troublesome or fatal malady. Most plant diseases spread to others of the same species or variety. Some spread rapidly and some slowly. A great difference will be found in the disease-resisting powers of different varieties, and sometimes one variety will be proof against a disease which has ruined another variety growng in close proximity. While this immunity may exist in the case of certain varieties, it is nevertheless not wise to give any form of plant disease an opportunity to spread. Plants that have been dug or pulled up on account of disease or apparent weakness from any cause, should be burned at once. This is the most convenient and the surest way of destroying disease germs or equally destructive insects wihch may infest the plant. Anthracnose is a common ailment of the raspberry, particularly the black varieties. This affects the canes, which take a spotted appearance. This affection has not been troublesome here. Burn affected canes and treat with Bordeaux mixture. **Curl Leaf** has been observed amongst raspberries here. The first indication is a curling of the leaves. Later the leaves dry and the affected cane dies. The fruiting canes are first affected and the maturing crop is usually destroyed or of very poor quality. Later in the season the new canes are affected. Burn affected plants. Red or orange rust is another disease of the raspberry, affecting the foliage. It is first noticeable by a sickly appear-

RASPBERRIES.

ance of the plants, and later a bright colored rust will be found on the under side of the leaves. Spraying with the usual fungicides is a preventative. Cutting and burning plants as early as possible is desirable. While very little trouble has been experienced from any of the raspberry affections in these provinces, it is well to be on the watch, and to know how to detect and overcome them.

INSECTS—There are many insects which attack the raspberry. A recent bulletin prepared by the Minnesota State entomologist gives a list of eighteen different insects which are troublesome to the raspberry. Several of these are cane borers, the remedy for which is to cut out and burn affected canes, while the insects in some form are present. Affected canes can usually be readily located. When the insect bores or punctures the new growth, the cane will usually assume a drooping and wilted appearance. Paris green sprays kill all leaf-eating insects. So far we have had little trouble from raspberry insects in our prairie provinces.

VARIETIES—There are a great many good varieties of raspberries offered, especially of the red sorts, but the number of really hardy varieties, viewed from the standpoint of our climatic conditions, is not extensive.

TURNER—The best known variety here. A red berry of medium size and excellent quality. Fruit rather soft for shipping, but perhaps the best berry for home use or local market. First degree of hardiness.

PHILADELPHIA—Equal to Turner in hardiness and one of the most prolific fruiters known, but not of first-class quality. Fruit medium size, purplish red color, soft and of indifferent flavor.

DR. REIDER—A variety which resembles Turner, but not as fine quality and not quite as hardy, though it may be classed as a hardy sort.

LOUDON—A very fine berry, both in quality and large size. Dark crimson color. Equal to Reider in hardiness.

SHIPPER'S PRIDE—Medium size, bright red, firm fruit. A good shipper, but of secondary quality. Very hardy.

KING—A new red variety of promise, but not tested long enough here to report upon with definiteness.

MINNETONKA IRONCLAD—A new Minnesota variety which has rapidly become very popular. Fruit large, crimson color, firm and excellent quality. A heavy cropper and hardy. The canes are of a drooping habit, somewhat resembling the Philadelphia.

CUTHBERT—A well known variety which has been largely grown for years in the East, but not hardy enough for extensive planting here.

MARLBORO—An early red variety, desirable for market. Large fruit, of secondary quality. Fairly hardy.

GOLDEN QUEEN—This is the best yellow berry, but it is tender and will require very careful winter protection. Several growers about

Winnipeg claim to succeed well with this variety. The Caroline is a much hardier yellow variety, but not of as good quality.

PURPLE VARIETIES—Some growers claim to have had good results from Schaeffers, but there is no purple variety that we can recommend for general planting. The Schaeffer is a tip-rooting variety.

BLACK VARIETIES—There are quite a number of good tip-rooting varieties. In selecting these the low growing sorts are perhaps best adapted to our climate. The strong, tall growing varieties are difficult to cover, and all need protection. Older and Ohio are two good varieties which meet the requirements as to low growth.

CHAPTER V.
BLACKBERRIES.

Among the many inquiries which have come to the writer regarding fruit growing in these provinces, a sprinkling have related to the blackberry. Generally speaking this question can be answered by the statement that the blackberry is not adapted to the prairie provinces of Western Canada. While some varieties of the blackberry are perhaps as hardy as many varieties of the raspberry, yet I have never heard of any one succeeding in growing this fruit. The fruit is later in ripening than the raspberries, and will usually not mature here before fall frosts set in. These remarks apply to the upright form of the blackberry. There is a recumbent or trailing form of blackberry which ripens its fruit considerably earlier than the erect forms. As the vines trail naturally along the ground, they are easily covered, and should be well mulched for winter. These trailing forms, known generally as dewberries, are not nearly as largely cultivated as the upright varieties. They produce very fine, large fruit, but are not generally considered sufficiently productive to be profitably grown as a commercial crop. The fruit of the dewberries ripens here and they may be grown with good winter protection. The upright varieties require the same general treatment as the raspberry. Blackberries are sometimes confounded with black raspberries. They are closely related to the raspberry, botanically, but are a different species. Their manner of growth is the same as the suckering raspberries. The recumbent forms are propagated by layering the new canes. Both the upright and recumbent forms of blackberries are natives of the northern States and the milder parts of Canada. The upright varieties generally cultivated belong to the species **Rubus villosus** and the dewberries to the species **Rubus Canadensis**. Ancient Briton, Snyder and Badger are well known upright varieties. Windom and Lucretia are recumbent sorts. Blackberries are grown very largely in some parts of the eastern States. Where they can be grown to advantage they are well worthy of cultivation, but in our climate the upright sorts at any rate should be planted only for experimental purposes.

CHAPTER VI.
BUFFALO-BERRY.

The Buffalo-berry, botanically known as **Shepherdia argentea**, is a shrub of light or silvery foliage. The flowers are inconspicuous and appear very early in the spring. It is an exceedingly hardy shrub, standing both exposure to low temperature and drouth well. It is a native of the wind-swept plains of Dakota and other sections of the Northwestern States, and is also found in sections of the Canadian prairie region. The fruit much resembles the red currant in appearance and flavor, but has only one seed, which is considerably larger than the currant. It is an abundant fruiter. It is not largely grown for fruit, but is worthy of trial, particularly in severe or dry locations. The shrub belongs to the class known as dioecious, that is, one plant will produce only pistillate or female flowers and another only staminate or male blossoms. In order to produce fruit, it is necessary that both male and female plants should be placed in proximity. Plants grown from the seed will usually be about equally divided in sex. The fruit is produced on short spurs and hangs well to the tree. The Buffalo-berry is a fine ornamental shrub, useful for lawns, borders or hedges.

CHAPTER VII.
RUSSIAN MULBERRY.

The Russian mulberry has been frequently tried here, but the tree invariably freezes back to the ground or to the main stem every winter. We know of no case where this tree has been cultivated here with success. It is grown to a considerable extent in Southern Minnesota, which appears to be about its northern limit of successful culture.

CHAPTER VIII.
CRANBERRIES.

We know of no attempt to cultivate the cranberry **(Vaccinium)** in any part of Manitoba or our other western provinces. As the plant is found growing wild and fruits well in some sections of this region there would appear to be reason to believe that it could be cultivated successfully in certain localities. The cranberry is not adapted to garden or general cultivation, as will appear from the remarks following. The cranberry is a swamp or bog plant, and will not, as a rule, thrive out of its natural habitat. Where it is found growing naturally, it can usually be cultivated successfully, provided the facilities exist for controlling the water supply, and draining and cultivating the land. The cranberry requires an abundant supply of water, and this water supply should be so controlled that the water can be drawn off when necessary to about a foot below the surface. While some natural cranberry bogs have been improved at moderate expense, it is generally a matter of considerable outlay to properly prepare the land for this crop. It would, therefore, be advisable for any one who contemplates entering upon this work, to study the situation carefully. Books specially devoted to cranberry growing may be obtained. These remarks have no reference to the so-called high bush cranberry. The latter shrub, which is very common in this country, is a viburnum, and not related to the genuine cranberry. There are several forms of the cranberry native to eastern Manitoba and the wood country to the north.

CHAPTER IX.

THE GRAPE.

Very little can be said as a result of practical experience regarding the cultivation of the grape in Manitoba or any other section of our prairie provinces. The cultivation of the grape is practically an unknown quantity here. A species of wild grape **(Vitis vulpina or Vitus riparia)** is found growing wild in the river valleys of southern and eastern Manitoba and the bordering territory of northwestern Ontario. It is a tall, strong growing climber. The fruit is produced in bunches of a purplish or bluish black color. After it has been subjected to frost the flavor of the fruit is fairly palatable, hence the common name Winter or Frost grape. The improvement of this native species may give us hardy grapes at some future date, well worthy of cultivation. This grape is now grown about Winnipeg to some extent as an ornamental vine, for which purpose it is well adapted. New varieties may be obtained by growing plants from seed, which should be sown in the fall in carefully prepared soil and mulched over winter. Some of the seedlings are likely to have imperfect flowers, and such will not be valuable for fruit experimental work. Cultivated grapes are usually propagated by cuttings from fruiting vines. These cuttings, of course, reproduce the parent vine.

The hardier varieties of grapes, grown in eastern Canada and the northwestern States, are of American origin, having been originated from the wild species botanically known as **Vitis labrusca**. This species is common in the northeastern States and is found as far west as eastern Minnesota. The improvement that has been effected in this species may indicate, to some extent at least, what possibly may be accomplished in the way of improving our own native grape. Many varieties of cultivated grapes are grown successfully in the more favored fruit sections of

THE GRAPE.

Minnesota, and Prof. Samuel B. Green, professor of horticulture in the Minnesota State University says that "there is probably no large section of Minnesota where some of the hardiest kinds of grapes cannot be grown and ripened." With this statement from Prof. Green before us, than whom no one is more competent to speak, we may well hope that some measure of success will ultimately be attained with the grape here, for there are sections of Manitoba which are perhaps better adapted to fruit growing than parts of Minnesota.

The cultivation of the grape requires rather more knowledge and skill than the growing of some fruits, and careful attention to pruning is necessary. The following simple directions, however, will be sufficient for those who may wish to experiment with this fruit.

SOIL AND PLANTING—The soil best adapted for the grape is a loose, loamy land, with good drainage. Our native grape is found on the heavy land of the Red River valley, but invariably in naturally well drained locations, such as the banks of ravines and streams. Two year old plants are best to begin with. No advantage is to be gained by using older plants for ordinary purposes. Plants should be set about eight feet apart. Plant deeply, especially on light soil, and leave a depression around the plant, which may be filled in gradually as the vine grows. Cut the top back to two or three buds before planting.

PRUNING—This is an important feature in the cultivation of the vine. The fall of the first year after planting cut the vine back to three or four buds. Mound the earth up around the root, completely covering the stub to a depth of several inches. This should be done before the plant has been subjected to sharp frost. Before severe weather sets in add a good mulch over the mound. This is important and its neglect will probably result in a loss of the plants. Uncover in the spring when danger of sharp frost is over and train the vine to stakes or a trellis. This may be done by placing posts ten to twelve feet apart and stretching wires along the posts. Allow one bud to grow and form the vine. At the end of the second season the main cane is again shortened back to about 3½ to 4 feet, and all lateral branches are cut off close to the main stem. The latter is then laid down on the ground and covered as in the previous fall. The following spring (third season) the cane is again uncovered and tied up to the lower wire, which should be about fifteen to eighteen inches from the ground. The three upper wires should be about ten inches apart. A number of lateral branches will start from the main cane. These should be pinched off when a few inches long, leaving only three or four of the strongest to extend upward. These are tied to the wires, and are usually pinched off when they reach the top. The vine may produce some fruit the third year, which will be improved in quality by the pinching process. In the fall of the third year the lateral branches are not cut off close to the main cane, as was done the previous fall. They are cut back, leaving three to six buds at the base of each spur or lateral. One lateral near the tip of the main cane may be left to extend the length of the main cane. If this is done, this lateral should be tied to the bottom wire the following spring the same as the main cane. This gives the permanent main cane for succeeding years. In the spring of the fourth year the main cane with extension, if any, is tied to the bottom wire, as just stated, and two or three shoots are allowed to grow from each spur, (that is, the lateral vines of the previous year, which were cut back to a few buds) the rest being pinched off. Three or four shoots may also be allowed to grow from the new extension of the main cane. This will give ten to about a dozen lateral vines for fruiting, which are pinched back at the tips when the desired height is reached. Each subsequent season the treatment is the same. The full length of the main cane having been attained, the laterals are cut back to the required number of buds each fall, and the vine is covered. The spurs from which the lateral vines start each spring, will be distributed along the main cane about eight or ten inches apart. There are other systems of training the grape. Sometimes two main canes, extending in opposite directions from the base of the plant, are allowed.

VARIETIES—In the absence of systematic efforts to cultivate the grape here, the only thing that can be said is to recommend the hardiest known varieties for trial. Professor Green recommends the following three varieties for the most severe localities of Minnesota: Janesville, Ives, and Hartford. A new grape, called the Beta, has been originated in Minnesota, which is possibly even hardier than the three named. A few of these are now under trial here. It has the advantage, for this climate, of ripening very early. Only a very early grape would be at all likely to succeed.

CHAPTER X.

THE APPLE.

The apple is the best known and most highly esteemed fruit of the temperate zone, and it reaches its highest state of perfection in moderately cold climates. With the apple, as with many other plants, the finest fruit is produced near the northern limit of profitable production. Most of the settlers of the new provinces of central and western Canada, came from regions where the apple is a well known crop. Naturally a desire to grow the fruit here formed a worthy ambition of a large number of our people. This has lead to the planting of a great many apple trees in Manitoba and other settled portions of the west. At the outset there was no data or experience available to serve as a guide to those who wished to plant trees. The work was carried on to a large extent blindly and in a haphazard manner. It is, therefore, not a matter for surprise that as a general thing, failure has been the result of a great deal of the planting of apples and other tree fruits. Our settlers early learned the lesson that the system of cultivation followed in the countries whence they came, would not answer in growing grain crops in their new homes. Special varieties were found best adapted to the country and systems of cultivation suited to our requirements were worked out. In horticulture the same principles apply. We must work out our own salvation here also, by finding or originating varieties suited to our needs, and learning the systems of cultivation suited to the country. In the matter of fruit growing and other horticultural work, we have been slower to learn this needful lesson than we have in growing grain or other field crops. Indeed, our people, or a great many of them, seem still to be ignorant of the first principles of successful fruit culture. The proof of this is the large quantity of worthless nursery stock annually brought into the country from the east, west and south. We say west advisedly, for shipments of nursery stock have actually been brought in from the mild and moist Pacific Coast climate, evidently under the absurd belief that such stock would grow here. A large portion of the apples, as well as other fruits and nursery stock annually brought in, belong to varieties which have been proved to be utterly worthless here. Yet there is a large crop of new victims each year. The late Peter Gideon, of Excelsior, Minnesota, who originated many of the best apples now grown in that state, relates his experience in the Thirteenth Annual Report of the Minnesota State Horticultural Society. The following extract is from that report:

"Our efforts and trials in Minnesota began thirty years ago last spring by planting one bushel of apple seed, a peck of peach seed, and five hundred apple, pear, plum and cherry trees, and for eleven years thereafter planting each year enough apple seed to bring 1,000 trees, and in the time named frequent additions to the orchard of old named varieties—all southern or eastern grown trees and seeds, and all kept as long as they could be made to live in Minnesota, and to-day only two trees remain. One of these is the Wealthy, from seed obtained of Albert Emerson, of Bangor, Maine, of whom I obtained scions at the same time, from which I grew the Duchess, Blue Pearmain, and the Cherry crab, all of which, combined, were the foundation of Minnesota horticulture, that to-day is the pride and hope of the Northwest. But since these varieties came into bearing we have planted only of our own growing of seed, with forty first-class varieties the result."

Here is a lesson for those who would plant fruit trees here or endeavor to produce new varieties suitable to this climate. It took thousands of trees and bushels of seed, brought from the east or further south, to produce one or two apple trees suitable for the Minnesota climate. But when it became possible to obtain seed of home-grown apples, forty good varieties were produced. Home-grown seed, if carefully saved, could be obtained here in considerable quantity, for originating new varieties.

Luther Burbank, who is called the wizard of horticulture, (an extravagant term, of course,), in speaking of the prospects of fruit growing in Minnesota, said that Minnesota would undoubtedly produce abundance of fruit, but, (and here is the important part of his remarks), he said, the work must be done in Minnesota. "It cannot be done elsewhere," he added. The work of growing hardy varieties and, if necessary, originating new varieties, and growing them under conditions adapted to the requirements of the planters of the state, must be done in Minnesota. If this is true of Minnesota, how much more is it true of our own more northerly provinces? In speaking of apple growing in Minnesota, Prof. Green, whom we have previously quoted, says: "It is far better that one should be entirely ignorant of the subject, but come with a desire to learn, than that he should undertake it with the belief that his experience in eastern orchard methods and varieties is sufficient to guide him in similar work here."

Of course much of the work done in the past by our settlers cannot be called mistakes. It could not be called a mistake to bring in apple trees when none could be had at home. A start had to be made somewhere. Experience could only be gained by practice and effort, where there was not the experience or advice of others to be secured. And so it has come about that through a great deal of planting and work, much carelessly and imperfectly done, but in some cases studiously and systematically followed up, we have gained considerable knowledge of apple planting in this country, and also at the same time some measure of success. Those who now wish to plant, can, if they wish, learn a great deal from the experience of others, which will materially assist them on the road toward success.

It cannot be said that the question of apple growing here has been solved, but it can be said that we are making progress in the right direction. We have learned a great deal as to the country. We know what are the hardiest and safest varieties to plant. But most important of all, we have trees now growing and annually producing fruit. This gives us a basis upon which to work for even better results in the future. The few trees which have proved hardy, out of the thousands which have been planted, are really the hope for the future. One tree which has been tested, and stood the test, is worth hundreds of untested trees. They are the trees which we should use from which to propagate our apples for future planting. These hardy trees can be increased by propagation by grafting, and new and possibly even hardier varieties may be obtained from them by planting the seed. This, then, is the promising outlook for the future. While many will continue to bring in trees which have been untried by our climate, and while this, at least from an experimental point of view, is commendable, the reproduction of the hardy trees which we now have, by grafting and growing seedlings, together with propagating from other hardy specimens which may later be discovered, will give our provinces the apples of the future.

The great majority of people who plant apple trees do not do it for the purpose of experimenting. They want to grow apples. To these the first and most important advice that can be given is: Secure trees, if possible, that have been propagated from trees that have been tested in our climate and stood the test. If such trees can be secured, this is the first and greatest step that can be made toward getting trees that will eventually produce apples. There is certainly some difficulty in securing such trees. The supply of home-grown trees is not large, and some of these are perhaps not propagated from the best specimens. Some that are sold as home-grown are perhaps really not home-grown at all. There is another way, however, to obtain trees besides purchasing the young trees from nursery growers. This is by top-grafting. The work of top-grafting is very simple. With a little practice any one would soon be able to perform the operation fairly well. The method is explained in the chapter on grafting. The first thing necessary is to secure the trees upon which to graft. Fortunately we have hardy varieties which may be grown for top-grafting purposes. The **Pyrus baccata**, or wild Russian crab, is thoroughly hardy. When these attain sufficient size they may be top-grafted successfully with the apple. A liberal planting of these hardy crabs should be made by those interested in apple growing. If cuttings, or scions as they are called, of hardy trees could be obtained, the trees would then be at hand upon which to graft them. In many of the older settlements cuttings from tested trees may be procured. One advantage of top-grafting is, that it ensures a hardy root and trunk. Top-grafted trees cannot be purchased, as they are too large to handle in this way. The trees for top-grafting must be grown where they are to remain after grafting. A hardy root and trunk is of great importance in growing the apple. They are perhaps the two weakest parts of the tree. The top-grafted tree, when a really hardy one, such as these crabs are, thus overcomes these two weak points. The apple is a stronger grower than the crab, and in some cases there may be danger that the graft will outgrow the tree on which it has been worked. Some of the hardiest hybrid apples, or seedlings of such hybrids, would be valuable for top-grafting with the stronger growing standard apples. The planting of hardy seedlings with the object of top-grafting them later on, need not interfere or check the planting of standard nursery trees. It would lead to the interesting of more people in horticultural work, and in districts where hardy trees had become established, it would assist in perpetuating and extending the usefulness of such trees.

SHELTER.—Shelter belts or windbreaks should be provided before any extensive plantings of apples or other tree fruits are made. It is particularly necessary to have good shelter belts upon the south and west sides, with moderate shelter on the remaining sides. The shelter belts will protect from warm, drying winds in summer, as well as prevent the blowing away of snow in the winter. Trees in fruit require protection from the wind, otherwise the crop is likely to be greatly reduced by wind-falls. Care, however, should be taken to so arrange the shelter belts that drifts of snow will not form about the trees. Many trees have been destroyed by drifts, the weight of the snow breaking off the branches, sometimes leaving only a bare trunk. Fruit trees should not be placed so near a shelter belt that they are robbed of the soil moisture by the sheltering trees. Willows and poplars take a great deal of moisture from the soil, and fruit trees must be at a respectable distance from shelter belts of these trees. They may be grown with safety much closer to a spruce shelter belt, but few of such shelters are available. For the same reason fruit trees are not likely to succeed planted in or near a natural woods. They are robbed of moisture by the surrounding trees and are so weakened that they are in poor condition to stand the winter. The loss of trees is undoubtedly a question of lack of moisture in many cases. The trees literally freeze dry. Hence the advisability of retaining moisture in the soil by good cultivation and mulching.

LOCATION—A northern slope undoubtedly presents special advantages for growing fruit trees, though some of the most successful attempts at growing apples have not had this advantage. It affords protection from the warm, drying winds which come from the south or southwest, and is not so much exposed to the full force of the sun's rays. The land should be well drained and somewhat elevated above the surroundings level, if possible. The apple seems to do particularly well on elevated locations, partly no doubt on account of the good natural drainage afforded. The healthiest trees, and therefore in the best shape to resist disease or severe changes of temperature, are usually found on the elevated spots. It is well known that elevated areas are less liable to suffer from frost. Small sheltered enclosures, which receive the full force of the sun during the day, while the tempering breeze is excluded, are not desirable places to plant apples or other tree fruits. Such spots are frequently selected by inexperienced persons on account of the shelter they afford. A location without shelter at all would be better. Such locations become excessively warm during the day. The trees are forced ahead in the spring, and suffer most from the sharp night frosts which often prevail at that season.

SOIL—The apple will thrive on soils varying widely in character, from light to heavy, providing other conditions are favorable. Our prairie soil is usually quite rich enough without manuring. Indeed, too rich soil is one thing to be avoided, as it has a tendency to prolong growth later in the season. It is desirable to have growth stop early in the season, so the wood may have time to harden up before severe weather sets in. Forcing growth by manuring is to be avoided.

SELECTING TREES—Many planters make the mistake of securing large trees. Trees two years old are the best. Older trees are not likely to do as well as trees of this age. The size of the tree is of less importance than a good root system. Fruit trees are either budded or grafted. That is, the named variety which is sold by the nurseries, is grown upon the root of a seedling tree. For our climate it is specially desirable that the seedling root should be of a hardy character. Apple trees as generally sold, however, are grown without any knowledge as to the hardiness of the roots. The seed for growing the roots is procured in the open market or obtained promiscuously by washing out the pomace from the cider mills. Both seed and roots are obtained to a considerable extent from Europe. Budding is commonly practiced in many of the Eastern and more southerly nurseries. In the northwestern states grafting is the common practice with the apple. This practice is preferable to budding for northerly districts. The graft is inserted in the root below the ground. If a long scion or graft is used and the root is planted fairly deep, the tree may eventually send out roots above the graft and thus become established on its own roots. In budded trees, the bud is inserted at or above the surface of the ground and as the root is quite likely to be tender, there is a liability of the tree killing below the bud. For our climate apples, whether budded or grafted, should be grown on hardy roots such as seedlings of the hardy crabs. This would obviate the danger of root-killing, which is a fruitful cause of loss when trees are exposed to a low temperature at a time when the ground is not well covered with snow. It is safe to say that very few of the tree brought into our provinces from the east or south possess the necessary hardiness of root. The possession of such hardiness would be the result of mere accident, as the way the roots are grown precludes any possible knowledge as to their hardiness. The variety or name by which the tree is known, therefore, does not indicate the hardiness of the entire plant. The hardiest variety obtainable may be grafted or budded upon a very tender root. This will explain why trees so frequently kill at the root. The measure of the hardiness of the tree, taking the root and all together, is the hardiness of the weakest part, and the weakest part is often the seedling root upon which the named variety has been worked. The strength of a chain is its weakest link. The hardiness of the tree is its weakest part.

PLANTING—Planting the apple should invariably be done in the spring. While trees may safely be procured in the fall, they should be "heeled in" over winter. Indeed there are decided advantages to be gained by securing the trees in the fall, some of which are referred to in the chapter on handling nursery stock. The general instructions regarding planting will apply to the apple. In average soil the trees may be planted from three to six inches deeper than they grew in the nursery, varying the depth according to the size of the tree and the nature of the soil. On very light soil they may be planted up to a foot deeper with safety. Deep planting affords protection to tender roots, assists the tree in forming roots above the graft, in which case the tree may eventually become on its own roots, and be independent of the seedling root. It also ensures moisture. There is, however, danger of overdoing deep planting on heavy soil, and sickly, delicate trees will be the result. In our climate, where a number of trees are to be set out, it is advisable to plant quite closely. The trunks are thus afforded a certain amount of protection from the sun. Sixteen feet is not too close, and in many cases fourteen feet will be sufficient distance between trees. The trees may be set so that the trees in the second row will stand opposite the vacant spaces or centres of the first row, and so on. Read the chapter on Planting for further information.

PRUNING—People who come from milder and moister climates are very liable to prune too much. Fruit trees here will require very little pruning. When the young trees are first planted they will usually require some thinning of the branches, and they should also be cut back by shortening the growth of the previous year about one-half. This will greatly assist the tree in becoming established in its new home. After that very little pruning should be done, except to cut out branches that interfere or rub. The best time to prune is when the shoots are so tender they can be pinched or rubbed off with the hand. For severe locations trees may be grown in bush form. In any case they should be trained to branch from near the ground. A long, bare trunk is objectionable. Such trees are very liable to suffer from sunscald. In low trimmed trees the branches shade the trunk and there is consequently less danger of sunscald. Suckers and water sprouts should be kept cut off. The term water-sprout is applied to rank sucker-like growths which start out from the trunk or large limbs of the tree. These should not be left until they attain large size, but should be rubbed off by the hand when quite small. If the trees are not pruned at all, nature will grow them in bush form, often with several sprouts starting from below the surface. In the nurseries the buds or sprouts are kept rubbed off, with the object of forming one straight central trunk, with the branches radiating therefrom. This makes a more symmetrical and useful tree for general purposes, but not as hardy as the bush tree. Where the trees can be grown on one main trunk, it is more satisfactory to have them in that form, but for this climate the trunk should be quite short. Nursery trees as usually supplied are trimmed too high for best results here. Providing the tree is worked on a hardy root, the trunk is its weakest part. It should be remembered that a tree does not grow from the trunk. While the trunk increases in circumference by the addition of layers of new growth, it does, not grow in length, therefore, the height of the branches from the ground will remain the same as where they have been first allowed to grow. Plants grow from the tips upward, outward or downward as the case may be, and not like the human arm, for instance, which increases in length between the joints. The tree may be pruned out a little more from the north or north-east side, to allow of easier approach from that side. The shading of the trunk is mainly desirable on the south or southwest. To increase the shade in this direction, the tree may be planted so that it will lean slightly to the south. Trees which lean to the northeast are more liable to sunscald. In this position the sun beats directly upon the trunk. A tree that leans to the south is not subjected to the full force of the sun's rays. Trees are sometimes damaged by the breaking or splitting of branches from storms. Split branches may often be saved by inserting an iron bolt through a crotch. A wire nail will sometimes answer the purpose, but for heavy limbs a long, thin bolt is better.

PROTECTION—Protection of the apple applies mainly to plans used to protect from sunscald, or the barking of the tree by mice or rabbits. Where the tree has been grown on a long, bare trunk, such protection is absolutely necessary, and even with such protection as can be provided, it is difficult to save the tree. Winding the tree with strips of jute or some other cloth is frequently practiced. The cloth is cut into strips about four inches wide. Starting at the ground this is wound around the trunk and tied at the top. Black cloth should not be used, as it is well known that the action of the sun is felt more keenly on black cloths. Tar paper should never be used. Wood veneers for wrapping the trunks of trees is commonly used. These can be purchased from nurserymen. Lath screens are made by wiring a number of laths together and wrapping them around the tree. Boxing is also practiced and perhaps affords the best protection to the trunk, if the box is filled with earth. Where trees are grown in bush form, or on very low trunks, some of these forms of wrappings are hardly applicable. Where mice are troublesome, banking around the base of the tree is a sure preventative of barking. This is also an additional protection to the roots. Rabbits have proved very troublesome in some localities, by cutting the limbs of small or low growing trees. They are very fond of the young apple wood. Spraying the trees in the fall with some liquid that would adhere to the bark and render the tree objectionable to the rabbits would be the easiest way of treating small or bushy trees, but no spraying mixture for this purpose has been suggested, though several chemists have been appealed to to suggest some liquid spray for such purpose. Trunk protectors are of no use against this form of damage. Sunscald usually occurs in the late winter or early spring, and is no doubt due to the alternate action of warm sun and frost. The effect of sunscald is to kill the bark on the side of the tree exposed to the sun. If trees are girdled by mice, they are greatly assisted in the healing process by being banked up with earth to cover the affected part. If this is not practical, they may be bandaged, first covering the wound with grafting wax, or even clay or fresh cow manure may be used. Where a tree is completely girdled they can usually be saved by inserting scions in the sound bark above and below the wound. Several of these may be inserted at intervals around the tree. Thus a connection is formed between the root and the top. The scions will grow rapidly and eventually cover the wound.

CULTIVATION—The ground planted to fruit trees should be kept well cultivated, the object in view being to preserve the moisture in the soil. For this purpose frequent surface cultivation should be kept up, particularly in the early part of the summer and up to the time that growth should cease. Grain or fodder crops, or any crops that will take much moisture, should not be grown among the trees. Vegetable crops may be grown and these should be planted in rows so the surface cultivation may be continued. Ground that becomes dry so that cracks open up in the soil, shows neglect of surface cultivation. Where a loose blanket of earth is maintained on the surface, no cracks to evaporate the moisture from the soil will be seen. In our dry climate, clean cultivation and a continuous loose surface or dust blanket is the best for the apple as well as other fruits. There is difference of opinion on this point. In milder and moister climates where apples are more largely grown, it is customary to sow a cover crop in the summer. This is allowed to remain on the ground to afford winter protection to the roots. This plan is advocated by some of our own horticulturists. In a wet season, the cover crop, if sown early enough, would take considerable surplus moisture from the soil and have a tendency to cause an earlier ripening of the wood. To this extent it would be an advantage. In our average season of dry summers and falls, the cover crop, by taking moisture from the soil, would do more harm than good. As for the winter protection afforded by the cover crop, it is a question if a good blanket of loose soil is not as good cover for winter protection as the cover crop would be. Cultivation early in the season will stimulate growth. In a very dry season cultivation may be kept up later. Late cultivation is supposed to keep the trees growing longer than is desirable, and retard the ripening of the wood. In a dry season it is not likely to have this effect. If it is thought desirable to sow a cover crop in a wet year, oats may be sown in July and allowed to remain until cultivation starts the following year.

MULCHING—Land worked on the clean cultivation plan will be benefitted by a mulch in the fall. It will prevent drifting of the soil, retain moisture and retard the freezing of the ground, all of which are of much advantage to the trees, by supplying moisture and preventing them from "freezing dry" in winter.

DISEASES—Twig blight is a common trouble in Minnesota and it has been observed here to a limited extent. This is the disease that kills the growing wood. It is supposed to be a germ disease. It is most noticeable in the early part of the summer, especially in seasons of rapid growth. Some varieties are much more subject to this disease than others. As soon as it is observed, the diseased branches should be cut out and burned, cutting some distance below the affected part. Instruments used for pruning may convey the trouble to other trees, and should be disinfected. Affected twigs dry up, and this is sometimes the first warning. Later in the summer the disease appears to stay its progress, but trees are often so badly damaged as to be practically ruined. Apple scab, which disfigures the fruit with black blotches, is prevented by spraying with Bordeaux mixture.

INSECTS—Apples, so far as grown here, have not been subject to attacks of insects to any extent. Borers have been discovered in a few cases. This is the larva of a small black or greenish beetle. The eggs are deposited under loose pieces of bark. The presence of borers may easily be detected late in the summer. Various washes for painting the trunk and large limbs are used, but they are not often necessary. Soft soap, mixed with a solution of washing soda, and reduced to the consistency of a thick paint, is applied with a brush. The borers may be cut out with a knife or killed with a piece of wire. All leaf eating insects, such as tent caterpillars, etc., are destroyed by Paris green, and for sucking insects use kerosene emulsion. Wormy apples are the result of the work of the Codling Moth. The moth lays its eggs in the calax or eye of the apple about or shortly after the petals fall. The young worm eats into the apple, and such apples become prematurely ripe. The early broods leave the apple, while late broods will be found in the apples during fall and winter. Spraying with Paris green after the blossoms fall is the usual remedy. Worms in the apples should be destroyed.

VARIETIES—The apple has been in cultivation so long that its early history to a great extent is unknown. There are a great number of varieties. The first parent of our cultivated apples is believed to be the **Pyrus malus**, which is a native of northern Europe and Asia. Farther north in Asia there is another species of wild apple or crab, called **Pyrus baccata**. This is represented in cultivation by the Siberian crabs. Most of our so-called crab-apples, however, are hybrids, originated from

THE APPLE.

crossing varieties of the **Pyrus malus** with the crabs. There are many other species of apples besides the two mentioned. Several species are native in Canada and the United States, but they have not been cultivated to any extent. No species of the apple family is native to our prairie provinces, though they are found in Eastern Canada, and also west of us in British Columbia. It only requires a limited experience to discover the difference between the growing apple tree and the crab, even when the trees are dormant. The new growth of the crab is smaller, smoother and harder than the apple. Leaves longer and smoother. Fruit hangs on longer and thinner stems; calyx usually drops from the matured fruit. The apple retains the calyx, has thicker leaves, somewhat wooly on the under side. Fruit stems short and thicker. New growth of wood thicker than the crab and wooly.

The apple was introduced to America from western Europe. Later, as settlement extended to the northwestern states, there was a demand for hardier varieties than those grown in the east. This demand has been to some extent met by the introduction of varieties from Russia. Our very hardy varieties are now of Russian origin. These Russian apples are mostly early varieties. The nomenclature of these Russian apples appears to have been very mixed. We have now several names for what are apparently the same varieties, or so nearly identical as to be very difficult to distinguish any difference. Some of the Russian apples are quite handsome in appearance. The mere fact that an apple may be classed as a Russian does not determine its hardiness. Many of them have proved too tender for Minnesota, and such would doubtless be useless here. For the benefit of those who may wish to experiment somewhat extensively in planting apples, we give herewith several lists of hardy varieties. It must be remembered, however, as already stated, that the variety does not decide the hardiness of the tree. If grafted on a tender root, the root is the measure of hardiness. The training and pruning of the tree, whether high or low trimmed, is also a factor in estimating its hardiness. The nature of the wood, as influenced by climatic conditions prevailing where the tree was grown, is a further consideration. A tree grown in a moister or milder climate would undoubtedly be unfavorably influenced in the growth of wood, for planting in a colder region.

List recommended for planting in the coldest districts of Ontario, as given in a pamphlet issued by the Department of Agriculture: Duchess, Hibernal, Wealthy, Longfield, Patten, Scott Winter, Charlamoff, Yellow Transparent, Whitney, Hyslop. The last two are hybrids.

List of the hardiest varieties for planting in colder districts of Ontario and Quebec, given in a bulletin prepared by W. T. Macoun, Horticulturist, Dominion Experimental Farm, Ottawa: Summer and fall apples—Tetofsky, Yellow Transparent, Duchess, Charlamoff, Wealthy, Hibernal, McMahon White, Longfield, Patten. Winter—McIntosh Red, Scott's Winter, Malinda, Milwaukee, Northwestern Greening. Hybrids—Whitney, Martha, Transcendent.

List recommended by Prof. N. E. Hanson, of the South Dakota Agricultural College, for the coldest section of that state: Hibernal, Duchess, Charlamoff, Wealthy. Hybrids—Martha, Virginia, Whitney, Sweet Russett, Lyman's Prolific, Brier Sweet, Mary.

THE APPLE.

List prepared by Prof. C. B. Waldron, of the North Dakota Agricultural College, for that state: Duchess, Hibernal, Charlamoff, Patten, Wealthy, Malinda. Hybrids—Virginia, Whitney, Early Strawberry, Minnesota, Gideon No. 6, Florence, Lyman's Prolific.

List for Minnesota, prepared by Prof. Samuel B. Green, of the University of Minnesota: Duchess, Borovinka, Charlamoff, Longfield, Hibernal, McMahon White, Wealthy, Breskovka, Thaler, Blushed Colville, Anisim, Patten, Malinda. Hybrids—Early Strawberry, Whitney, Minnesota, Transcendent, Martha, Virginia, Tonka, Pride of Minneapolis, Gideon No. 6, Sweet Russett.

List recommended by the Minnesota Horticultural Society: Duchess, Hibernal, Charlamoff, Patten (Patten's Greening is the same apple), Wealthy, Tetofsky, Malinda, Okabena, Peerless, Northwestern Greening. Hybrids—Virginia, Whitney, Early Strawberry, Minnesota, Sweet Russett, Gideon No. 6, Briar Sweet, Florence, Transcendent, Lyman's Prolific, Faribault, Shields. The society also gives the following supplementary list for trial: Repka Malenka, Anisim, Yellow Sweet, Brett, Scott's Winter, University, Newells, Lowland Raspberry, Estelline, Iowa Beauty, Jewell's Winter, Yahnke, Gilbert.

The following list was selected at a meeting of the Western Horticultural Society, held in Winnipeg, as the best varieties for this country: Standard apples—Hibernal, Duchess, Patten's Greening, Charlamoff, Anisette, Blushed Calville. Hybrid apples—Transcendent, Hyslop, Whitney, Virginia, Early Strawberry.

The apples named in the several lists given herewith will vary very materially in hardiness. Those who wish to plant for fruit should try only the very hardiest at first. Those who start in with the intention of doing some experimental work have a considerable range to select from. The hybrid apples will generally be found hardier than the standard varieties, but some of them are not as hardy as the hardiest standards. It is not to be expected that the hardiest apples in the lists will prove generally successful. Apple growing in these provinces is still more or less experimental. We have yet to find the varieties that can be recommended with confidence for all sections. While a few have met with some success in growing apples, many fail, much depending on the district where the planting is done.

In August, 1901, an exhibition of apples and plums grown in Manitoba was held in Winnipeg. A list of the apples shown on this occasion is given herewith, as follows: Sugar Sweet, White Rubets, Blushed Calville, Romna, Hibernal, Simbrisk No. 1, Red Cheek, Russian Gravenstein, Simbrisk No. 9, Borovinka, Cinnamon Pine, Saccharine, Repka Kislaga, Kluveskoe, Dula, Cross No. 15, Haas, Duchess, Silken Leaf, Ostrekoff, Little Hat, Kourisk Anis, Lieby, Grandmother, Charlamoff, October, Victor, Russian Green, Yellow Anis, Wealthy, Patten's Greening. Also the following crabs and hybrids: August, Whitney, Sweet Russet, Minnesota, Transcendent, Hyslop, Virginia, General Grant, Greenwood, Philip's 1,000, Orange, Beeche's Sweet, Briar Sweet, Dart, Martha, Tonka, Siberians. A number of seedlings produced in Manitoba were also shown.

This list of exhibits is possibly faulty in the naming of a few varieties, but it shows that even at that date quite a respectable exhibit of home-grown fruits could be made. More recent exhibits of fruit have been held, but a list of the exhibits is not available. Following is a brief description of the more desirable varieties:

HIBERNAL—This apple represents the extreme limit of hardiness so far as known of any apple. The Duchess is frequently given first place as to hardiness, but experience here is in favor of the Hibernal. The Hibernal is a Russian apple. Fruit large, greenish yellow, splashes of pale red, numerous white dots, medium fine flesh, season winter, acid, juicy, good for cooking. Tree vigorous, spreading, crooked grower. The best standard tree for top grafting with other varieties. Like many of the other Russian apples, there are several other so-called varieties which closely resemble or are possibly identical with the Hibernal. These are Lieby or Recumbent, Silken Leaf, Yellow Arcadian, etc.

DUCHESS—Also called Oldenburg or Duchess of Oldenburg. The best known and one of the best Russian sorts. Fruit large, round, greenish yellow, striped and streaked with red, numerous white dots, flavor sprightly acid, good; season fall. A summer apple farther south. Similar or almost identical varieties are: Arabian, Borovinka, White Krim, Anisovka or Anisette, Glass Green.

CHARLAMOFF—Origin Russia, fruit medium to large, light yellow, dark red or crimson stripes and splashes, dots white, flesh white, fine grained, agreeable acid, good. Season fall. A summer apple in southern Minnesota. Like most of the Russian apples, there has been a considerable mixing of names in connection with this apple. Two distinct apples have been brought from Russia and sold under this name. The one we have described is sometimes called Peterson's Charlamoff. The other apple has now been named Schroeder. The Charlamoff resembles the Duchess in color, but is more oblong. About as hardy as Duchess. Other varieties resembling or possibly identical are Pointed Pipka, Champagne, Champanskoe.

PATTEN'S GREENING—Originated by C. G. Patten, of Iowa, from seed of the Duchess, obtained at Portage, Wisconsin. The Minnesota Horticultural Society has placed this apple in the list with those of the first degree of hardiness. Fruit large, yellowish green, flesh white, juicy, sprightly sub-acid, good for table use or cooking. Season early winter. Resembles McMahon, but has green dots, while the latter has white dots.

ANISETTE or ANISOVKA—Resembles Duchess. Tree more upright habit, and ripens earlier than the Duchess.

BLUSHED CALVILLE—Origin Russia. Fruit medium size, yellowish white, with slight blush, dots white, flesh white, fine grained, juicy, good. A very early apple, and probably about as hardy as the preceding four varieties. Resembles Yellow Transparent.

BOROVINKA—See Duchess.

ANISIM—Origin Russia. Fruit rather small, greenish yellow, covered with dark red, dots white, flesh greenish white, good table apple. Season winter. Tree vigorous, healthy, hardy. This variety has many names, some of which are Zuzoff, Good Peasant, Boisdorfer, etc.

WEALTHY—Originated in Minnesota by Peter Gideon. It is said to have been grown from seed of the Cherry crab, but this is not credited by many horticulturists. As the seed was sent to Mr. Gideon from the State of Maine and passed through two or three hands, it is more than probable that it was of a mixed character. It is more probable that the Wealthy is a seedling of some apple of the snow family, than that it is a descendant of any crab. Fruit large, light yellow, covered with crimson splashes and stripes. A handsome apple of extra fine quality. The Wealthy is not as hardy as those previously dealt with, but is of superior quality. Trees of this variety have fruited in Manitoba, and it is worthy of trial in favorable locations. Classed by some authorities as hardier than Anisim.

CRABS AND HYBRIDS.

The crabs or hybrids vary much in quality, hardiness and healthfulness. Some of them partake more of the quality of the apple with which they have been crossed, than the crab.

TRANSCENDENT—This is the best known and most largely grown in the prairie provinces of any apple of its class. The tree is a strong, spreading grower and very hardy, but subject to twig blight in some localities. Fruit rich, yellow with reddish blush. Quality the very best for the purposes for which the crab is generally used, namely, jelly or canning. Not valuable for a table or dessert apple.

MARTHA—Originated in Minnesota. A very hardy, thrifty tree, not subject to blight. Fruit glossy yellow, shaded with red. Excellent for cooking or preserving. In some localities not an abundant bearer, but other growers pronounce it a good fruiter.

WHITNEY—Tree a strong, very upright grower. Fruit glossy green, splashed with carmine. A good desert apple, resembling more the apple than the crab.

HYSLOP—This variety is hardy, and produces showy dark crimson fruit. A late-ripening variety.

LYMAN'S PROLIFIC—A new variety that resembles Hyslop in color and shape, but of better quality and ripening earlier. This variety has rapidly become popular in Minnesota, where it was originated, and where it is a popular market fruit.

FLORENCE—Another tree of Minnesota origin. An early crab of excellent quality and handsome reddish fruit.

VIRGINIA—A strong, spreading grower. Fruit bright red. Season September-October.

EARLY STRAWBERRY—An excellent little apple for dessert or table use, but exceedingly perishable. Not suitable for market. Handsome appearance.

TONKA—A hardy Minnesota crab. Tree upright. Fruit acid. Good for cooking. Season, October-November.

SWEET RUSSETT—An early, sweet crab, useful for the table.

GIDEON NO. 6—A large, reddish crab. Season September. Good for cooking.

MINNESOTA—A large, yellow crab of good table quality. Keeps well.

SIBERIAN CRABS—There are two varieties of these, called the Red and Yellow Siberian. They are small true crabs, and somewhat astringent. The tree is exceedingly hardy. Trees loaded with this fruit in the most unfavorable seasons have been observed. They are closely related to the **Pyrus baccata,** of which they are probably selections.

The four hardiest of these crabs or hybrids, exclusive of the Siberian, are the Martha, Transcendent, Hyslop, Virginia. Wm. Saunders, L.L.D., Director of the Dominion Government Experimental Farms, Ottawa, has produced a large number of hybrids by crossing various hardy standard apples with the small **pyrus baccata.** Many of these have been planted at various points throughout the prairie provinces. Some of them at least will no doubt prove hardy, and add useful varieties to our list of desirable trees.

CHAPTER XI.

PLUMS.

The plum is sometimes spoken of as the tree fruit of the north. This is true of this continent so far as wild plums are concerned, for native plums are abundant in some sections of Manitoba, while no species of apple is found in this latitude. But while we have plums indiginous to the country, efforts to grow cultivated species and varieties of plums here have not met with as favorable results as has been the case with apples. The plums grown in the milder portions of Canada—parts of Ontario and British Columbia—belong mainly to the European species known as **Prunus domestica.** This plum has been under cultivation for centuries and has been brought to a high state of development. There are a great many varieties of this species in cultivation. During more recent years a number of varieties of the Japan plum have been introduced, some of which are hybrids resulting from crossing with the European species. No varieties of either of these species are of any value here. They have not been a success even in southern Minnesota.

There are quite a number of distinct species of wild plums found throughout North America. The two most northerly species are **Prunus nigra,** which is a native of Manitoba and bordering states, and **Prunus americana,** which occurs throughout the northern states, extending from Canada southward over a large area of territory. Inability to grow the European plum has no doubt increased the efforts in the northwestern states to improve the native plums, with the result that within a comparatively few years a great many selected varieties of the **Prunus ameri-**

cana have been been named and put on the market. A few named varieties of **Prunus nigra** have also been introduced. Varieties belonging to these two species are the only plums which have been found of any value here. A great many of the varieties of **Prunus americana**, however, do not ripen in this latitude. Many of these varieties have originated from the wild plums of southern Minnesota, Iowa and thereabouts, and while in some cases the trees have proven fairly hardy here, the fruit is often destroyed by the frost before it is sufficiently matured to be of any value. The De Soto, for instance, which is one of the oldest, best known and most largely grown in the northwestern states of the **Americana** class, will not ripen here in our most favored sections once in a dozen years. Only the very early varieties of this species should be selected for trial here.

Prunus nigra is so called from the dark color of the bark. It is rather a smaller tree than **Prunus americana,** and of more upright, or less spreading habit. It blossoms very early, and on this account is liable to suffer from spring frosts. The fruit varies widely in quality in its wild state, some being of fair quality and other trees producing exceedingly astringent fruit. Some trees will be found with ripe fruit in August, and others do not ripen except in very favorable seasons. The native plums are usually red, or purplish red in color, but occasionally yellow or splashed with yellow. The future of plum growing here will depend largely upon the improvement of our native plums, and the introduction of the hardiest of the early **americana** varieties. Many new varieties no doubt will be evolved, which will be suited to our climate.

PROPAGATION OF THE PLUM—New varieties are produced by growing from seed. Named varieties are usually propagated by budding, though sometimes by grafting. For our climate they should be grown only on roots of the native wild plum, whether budded or grafted. Plums of the **americana** class brought in from the bordering states to the south, are very liable to root-kill here. A great many have been lost on this account, owing to the use of roots that are much too tender for our climate. Until we have a sufficient supply of trees budded or grafted on our own native wild plum roots, planters of this fruit in our prairie provinces cannot hope for really satisfactory results. So for nearly all the plums planted here have been brought in from the south or east, and practically all of these are grown on roots that are quite too tender for our climate. Where such plums have been planted, the ground about them should be heavily mulched in the fall, to protect the roots.

PLANTING—Plums thrive best on well drained land, and high ridges, though they do well on retentive soils. They may be planted about ten feet apart in the rows, and several varieties should be planted together. This greatly assists in fertilizing the blossoms. Some varieties are not fruitful when planted alone. While the flowers are perfect in themselves, cross fertilization by other varieties is desirable and usually results in increased productiveness. Where a number of trees are growing in proximity, this cross-fertilization will be accomplished by bees or other insects, and the wind. Heavy, or dashing cold rains, during the blossoming period, sometimes operate to prevent the fertilizing of the plum to the extent desirable. Directions for the cultivation of the apple will apply to the plum. For the hardy native varieties, it is safe to allow a longer or higher trunk than is recommended for the apple, as they are not nearly as liable to sunscald. Very high trunks, however, are not desirable. Two to three feet is quite sufficient.

INSECTS—The most troublesome insects to the plum here are the small plant lice or aphis. Wild plum trees will frequently be found with an immense number of these insects upon the under side of the leaves, towards the tips of the branches, and on the young, soft wood. When in such large numbers they are very injurious to the trees. They should be treated by spraying with kerosene emulsion, which should be used early in the season. When they become very abundant, as they sometimes do, spraying is not always satisfactory in results. A decoction of steeped tobacco stems is useful for spraying to destroy the aphis.

PLUM POCKET—The **americana** and **nigra** plums are subject to several diseases of a fungous nature. That called Plum Pocket is perhaps the most common. This affects the fruit early in the season. The fruit swells out as though inflated by air, and when broken will be found to be only a thin shell with no pit nor seed. Later the "pocket" turns black. Trees will be found upon which practically the whole crop has been destroyed by this fungus. Spraying the trees early in the spring, before the buds open, with Bordeaux mixture, about double strength, is the remedy recommended. This strong solution must not be used after the tree is in leaf. The foliage of the plum is more tender than many other trees and will hardly stand the ordinary strength Bordeaux mixture. The pockets should be gathered and burned, as they may spread the spores.

SHOT HOLE FUNGUS—This fungus disease is difficult to control. It attacks the leaves and is easily recognized by the innumerable small perforations in the leaves. It begins with small spots upon the leaves. The diseased part eventually dries and drops out, leaving the perforations noted. It is very injurious to the trees, preventing the maturing of buds and the new growth of wood. Spraying, to be effectual, must be started early and repeated three to five times, sometimes even then without entirely satisfactory results.

BLACK KNOT—The plum, or at least many species of this fruit, are subject to attacks of the Black Knot. The European plum is very subject to it—much more so than our native plums. The wild chokecherry is very subject to the trouble. Thickets of the cherry have been observed in Manitoba which were almost completely covered with black knot, while an occasional plum tree among the cherries would be free from knots. The disease usually starts on the smaller limbs. In the spring the disease takes the form of greenish yellow swellings on the limbs. Later the knots turn black. Trees should be searched and the diseased limbs cut out and burned before the spores escape and are scattered by the wind. Knots on large branches or on the trunk may be brushed with kerosene. Wild cherry thickets are mainly responsible for the presence of the black knot. Spraying with strong Bordeaux mixture before the buds open, and with reduced strength later, will hold this disease in check.

VARIETIES—Prunus nigra—The two best known varieties of this species are Aitkin and Cheney. The former is a very large, red plum, yellow flesh. Not astringent, but lacks high quality. Ripe toward end of August. Cheney not as large as Aitkin, red, juicy, good quality. Season a little later than Aitkin.

AMERICANA VARIETIES—Only the very early sorts should be tried. Forest Garden, Wolf, Odegard, Bixby, Mankato are early varieties, but in the absence of extensive trials it is difficult to speak as to their relative hardiness. The lists recommended by the Minnesota and Dakota experts contain varieties which will not ripen in the most favored sections of Manitoba, so that it would be useless to give them here. Surprise is a new variety originated in Minnesota, which is becoming the most popular one in that state. Medium early.

CHAPTER XII.

CHERRIES.

No cultivated variety of tree cherry has been found that is of any real value here. Several attempts have been made to grow cherries, and a few trees have actually produced a sample of fruit in the more favored districts of eastern or southeastern Manitoba. These experiments, however, have had no practical value, except to indicate that the known varieties of cherries cannot be grown to advantage. A few varieties of cherries are grown in Southern Minnesota and the southern portion of South Dakota, but north of that latitude they have not been a success. The hardiest varieties of the cultivated tree cherry have been introduced from eastern Europe and are commonly spoken of as Russian cherries. To this class belongs such varieties as Ostheim, Bessarabia, etc.

There are several species of cherries native to the prairie provinces of Canada. These include **Prunus pennsylvanica** (Pin Cherry), which is found in wood sections all over the country. The fruit is very small but of good flavor. Color red. **Prunus demisa** is the common wild black or choke cherry. Fruit small and astringent. **Prunus pumila** is the bush or sand cherry. The fruit of this low growing species is larger than either of the others and varies much more in quality and size. Some is very bitter or astringent, but occasionally a plant will be found which produces a much better quality of fruit. The improvement of this species offers the best prospects for the future of cherry growing in our provinces. It is extremely hardy and quite prolific under cultivation. Plants that have been subjected to severe frost when in blossom have produced good crops. As a resister of spring frosts, it is surpassed by few fruits. Experiments in cultivating the bush cherry have been carried on quite extensively in Manitoba, Minnesota and Dakota, and some very fair fruit has been produced. So far, however, no named varieties have been offered, but plants grown from seed may be obtained from some of the nurseries. This cherry, like the apple and plum, does not come true from seed, and such seedlings would doubtless vary much in quality. Plants may be grown by budding, or by suckers, and such would come true to the plant from which they were taken. Suckers from a budded plant, however, would reproduce the root stock, and not the variety budded thereon. The bush cherry may be grown on our native plum roots, and the plum will also grow on the roots of this species of cherry. This cherry may also be crossed with the plum. Some crosses of this nature have been made in Minnesota. The so-called Compass cherry is a cross of this nature. The Compass cherry may now be obtained from some of the nurseries. The foliage resembles the cherry. Fruit red, oblong, and with the plum flavor to some extent. Size of an average native plum. Fair quality for canning. It ripens here early in September and the tree is fairly hardy.

CHAPTER XIII.

OUR NATIVE FRUITS.

It has repeatedly been asserted, sometimes by persons of experience, that the wild fruits of our prairie provinces are of better quality and more prolific than similar or related species of the east. Most of the cultivated fruits of the north are represented here by native species. Strawberries, raspberries, gooseberries, currants, cherries, plums, grapes, are all represented by one or more native species. The apple alone is not a native in any form. All our cultivated fruits have originated from wild species. Some of these have been under cultivation so long that their early history is unknown. Other forms of cultivated fruits, such as the American varieties of grapes, gooseberries and plums, are of quite modern origin. Some of our native fruits belong to the same species from which have been originated many cultivated varieties. This is true of our cultivated strawberries, suckering varieties of raspberries, and the American varieties of gooseberries, the parent species of which are native to our woods and prairies. Some of our native fruits are said to be of superior quality to the original form of some of the highly developed fruits of Europe. The European gooseberry and plum, both of which are now represented by numerous varieties of unsurpassed excellence, are said to be inferior in their original wild form to our native species. With this knowledge before us, there would seem to be no reason why some species at least of our wild fruits should not form the basis from which many fine cultivated varieties will in time be evolved. To talk of our provinces as a fruitless region, in view of the existence of all these native species, seems ridiculous. We have with us, hardy, fully acclimated native species, we may say, of nearly all the desirable northern fruits, the apple, as stated, being the one important exception. Here, then, is the great field for experiment. While we should use such cultivated fruits that come to us from other regions, as we find suitable for cultivation, our native fruits should not be overlooked. It should be possible to develop from these native fruits varieties equal in quality to many of the best cultivated sorts, while retaining the natural hardiness of a fully acclimated species. The work of plant breeding is expensive and uncertain in results, and should not, perhaps, be left to private enterprise alone. The individual who devotes his time to such employment is really working for the community at large, or, in other words, the state. This should not deter those who have opportunity to do what they can in the improvement of our fruits.

Reference has already been made in these pages to the improvement of our native fruits, in the chapters devoted to the cultivated fruits. One of our most promising native fruits is the plum, from which good results should be obtained by selection and breeding. The native plum is cultivated to some extent, mainly in the form of selected trees taken from the woods, but no named varieties have yet been offered which have been originated here by breeding. Some very good forms have been secured through selection. The possibility of evolving something good from our native species is discussed in the chapter on Plums. The native grape is referred to in the chapter on Grapes. Special chapters have been devoted to the Cranberry **(Vaccinium)** of which there are several forms, of excellent quality, and the Buffalo Berry. In the chapter on cherries, reference is made to the native species of this fruit. The Sand or Bush cherry **(prunus pumila)** is one of the most promising of our native fruits. It is adapted to severe locations, will thrive on poor soil, and resist severe drouth. Of strawberries there are two native forms, **Fragaria virginiana,** from which have originated most of our cultivated species, and **Fragaria vesca,** the woodland species. The raspberry is represented by **Rubus strigosus,** from which species have originated most of the cultivated varieties of red raspberries. There are three or four other native forms of the raspberry family, including an herbaceous dewberry, the dwarf Arctic raspberry, and a species growing very far north which produces yellow fruit. All four varieties have a wide distribution.

The gooseberry is represented by two species, of which **Ribes hirtellum** is one. From this species have originated several of the best cultivated varieties of American origin. Some of the native plants, selected from the woods, are cultivated by the settlers in some sections, and some plants producing fruit of very good quality have been found. The further improvement of this species, to supply the demand for a hardier gooseberry than we now have, is greatly to be desired.

Wild currants are found in nearly all sections of the country where there is any brush or forest growth. The black currant **(Ribes americanum)** is the more common form, and is cultivated to a considerable extent by the settlers. It is of good quality and size, but irregular in ripening The native red currant is closely related to our cultivated red varieties **(Ribes rubrum.)**

The Juneberry **(Amelanchor canadensis)** is found in river valleys, or wherever there is any forest growth, in nearly all sections of the country. It is also locally known as the Saskatoon berry. Some cultivated varieties of this fruit are offered by the nurseries, of which the

Success Juneberry is perhaps the best. It is, like the best of the other cultivated sorts, a dwarf variety. The dwarf form appears to offer better prospects for cultivation. The birds are very fond of this berry, and this fact has been a considerable source of discouragement to the cultivation of the fruit.

Viburnum opulus, commonly called the High Bush Cranberry, is a very common native fruit of considerable economic value. Plants for cultivation may be taken from the woods. It thrives on moist, retentive soils, and should receive about the same cultivation as other bush fruits of the garden. The fruit makes an excellent jelly, but for this purpose the berries should be gathered when they are quite firm. If left until the fruit becomes soft, it is difficult to make a good jelly from it The fruit also makes a good sauce, when put through a colander to remove the seeds and skins.

Blueberries are found in the rough rocky region bordering Manitoba on the east and in the northern sections of the three prairie provinces. Tons of this fruit are annually gathered and sent to the nearest markets. The Winnipeg market is liberally supplied in the shipments from the eastern portion of the province and the bordering region of northwestern Ontario. The fruit finds a ready sale at remunerative prices. Growing as it usually does on rough, poor land, it is perhaps not as well adapted to cultivation in the rich soil of the prairie districts as most of our other native fruits.

CHAPTER XIV.

PROPAGATING FRUITS FROM SEED.

Generally speaking, new varieties of fruits are obtained by growing from seed. Our cultivated fruits do not come true from seed. When it is desired to obtain new varieties in this way, cross fertilization or hybridization are usually resorted to with a definite object in view. Cross fertilization is the term applied to the crossing of two varieties of the same species. Hybridization is the crossing of two distinct species. The latter is the more difficult. Some species resist attempts to cross with others of the same family. In most cases, however, it is possible to cross different species of the same family, such as the apple **(Pyrus maulis)** and the crab apple **(Pyrus baccata).** In the chapter on cherries mention is made of the crossing of the native cherry and the Americana plum. The plum and cherry are related, botanically, both belonging to the genus Prunus. Cross-fertilizing or hybridizing may be carried out on the same general principles as would characterize like efforts in animal husbandry. Best results are likely to be attained when the work is carried on systematically and intelligently with a definite object in view. Naturally varieties combining the qualities sought in the new variety would be selected for cross fertilization. For instance, if a very hardy apple is desired, it might be necessary to select an inferior apple

PROPAGATING FRUITS.

of great hardiness to cross with a less hardy apple of good quality, the object being to combine the hardiness of the one with the good quality of the other, in the offspring.

Cross-fertilizing is not such a difficult operation that it may not be undertaken by any one of ordinary intelligence, possessing a reasonable knowledge of plants. The operation, briefly, consists in fertilizing the blossoms of one plant with the polen taken from another plant. Many of our plants possess both the male and female organism in the one blossom. If such are left to nature, they may become self-fertilized. In such plants it is necessary to remove the anthers (the vessels containing the pollen) from the blossoms to be operated upon, before they burst and scatter the polen. The polen from another plant is then applied with a small brush or other instrument to the pistil of the plant from which the anthers have been removed. The flowers are then cov-

Section of Young Seedling Apple Orchard at Buchanan Nurseries
St. Charles, Manitoba.

ered with gauze to prevent the introduction of polen from another plant by insects or otherwise. If the operation is successful and seed is obtained, the plants raised from this seed should in some measure combine the characteristics of the parents.

It is not necessary, however, to undertake any delicate or extensive work in cross-fertilizing in order to help on the work of developing our fruit growing interests. Seeds may be planted with some hope of obtaining good results, without undertaking cross-fertilization by hand. Seeds of home-grown apples, crabs, selected plums, etc., should be planted largely. Everyone who is able to secure any such seeds and who has a place to plant them should engage in the work. There are sufficient apples now grown here, if the seed were saved and planted, to produce an enormous number of seedlings, and some of these would surely prove valuable additions to the varieties we now have—probably hardier and better than those we now have. This is the way our fruit interest must be developed. The varieties that will be grown in the future will be produced here. More southerly countries can go north to secure suitable varieties, but a northern country cannot go south and hope for the best results. There is no more northerly country whence we can obtain hardy fruits. We must produce the varieties here. The object of this chapter is, therefore, mainly to give instructions for growing fruits from seed.

Seeds of small fruits, such as strawberries, raspberries, currants, gooseberries, etc., are best handled by being squeezed or rubbed out in sand. The fruit selected for seed should be fully ripe, and the seed should be sown at once in well prepared soil. Soil with an admixture of sand is best. Heavy soil is liable to bake and does not make a good seed bed. Strawberries will grow the first year if conditions are favorable, but the seed of most other varieties will not sprout until the following spring. Shading the seed bed is desirable, but is not absolutely necessary. The ground should be mulched in the fall, though in a sheltered place and with a good covering of snow, this is not always necessary. If growth starts early in the spring, the young plants may be destroyed by late frosts. The mulch will retard too early growth. After attaining one season's growth, the plants may be taken up and set out in rows to fruit. They should be well protected, especially the first winter, by covering strawberry plants with litter, and covering all woody plants entirely with earth, by banking up; or, if large, bending down and covering, and banking well around the roots.

Seeds of grapes and apples succeed best planted in the fall, if the soil is suitable. They may be planted considerably deeper than the small seeds of the other fruits. A light, friable, well drained soil is best. Mulch in the fall, and if there is a tendency of the soil to crust or bake in the spring, after the mulch is removed, rake it over with a steel rake. Watch for cut-worms, which often destroy all the young plants before their presence is noticed. The best remedy for cut-worms is poisoned bran. Sweeten and moisten bran, and poison with Paris green. The worms eat this greedily and are destroyed. Seeds that are secured during the winter or too late for fall planting, may be placed in a box with moist sand and put out doors to freeze. In the spring the sand is sifted out and the seeds are planted in the usual way. If liable to dry out, the box in which seeds are kept should be covered with straw or litter. It is sometimes necessary to shade the young plants to prevent "damping off." This is a fungus disease which causes the plants to rot off at the surface. This usually occurs shortly after the plants have appeared above ground, and is very destructive. A convenient shade is made of laths nailed upon strips of boards, leaving spaces the width of a lath alternately with each lath. These lath screens are placed over the seed beds. It is a good plan to protect seed beds by placing boards about 10 inches high, on each side of the bed. These are held up by stakes. In good locations it is not always necessary to use the screens, and they are only required while the plants are quite small. If the weather is very dry, watering may be necessary. If this is done at all a good soaking should be given. The custom of giving light waterings frequently is injurious and often more injurious than drouth. Young trees should be taken up in the fall and "heeled in" over winter. In the following spring they may be planted out where they are to be left to fruit. Seedling fruits for testing may be planted about six feet apart for apples and plums, and the poor ones cut out as they fruit. Weak trees, or those showing signs of disease or winter damage, should be cut out.

Plums and cherries require much the same general treatment as apples, but greater care is perhaps necessary to prevent the seed from becoming dry. The seed should be washed and planted soon after it is taken from the fruit. By observing this rule most of the seed will grow the first year. If planted late in the fall, much of the seed will remain in the ground over the second winter before it grows. Young seedlings of all kinds should be well cultivated both before and after transplanting to permanent rows. The soil should never be allowed to bake or crust and no grass or weeds should be allowed to grow among them. Plum and similar hard, bony seeds may be kept over winter by mixing in a box with damp sand and burying in the ground over winter. They should be planted early in the spring. Many of them will not grow until the second year after planting.

CHAPTER XV.

GRAFTING AND BUDDING.

The most rapid and least expensive mode of propagating plants is usually by growing from seed. Some plants do not come true from seed and it is, therefore, necessary to use some other mode of perpetuating them. This is accomplished in various ways, by separation, as in the removal of the small bulbs which form about the base of parent plants; by division, as in cutting up a potato into several parts; by layers and cuttings; and by grafting and budding. All our tree fruits are propagated in the latter way. Many ornamental trees and shrubs are also propagated by budding or grafting. The principle of grafting and budding is essentially the same. In grafting a small twig, carrying usually two to four buds, is used. In budding a single bud without any considerable attachment of wood is used. The tree or root upon which the operation is performed, is called the stock. The twig which is inserted is called the scion in grafting, or the bud in budding. In either grafting or budding, portions of two separate plants are united to form a new plant. The bud or graft becomes the fruitful portion of the tree, while the stock is only used as a means of propagating or perpetuating the variety from which the bud or graft was taken. The operation succeeds best on closely related species. That is when the scion and stock belong to the same or some closely related species. There are some divergencies, however, in this rule. The stocks upon which the operation of budding or grafting is performed are grown from seed.

GRAFTING—There are a great many different ways of grafting. The scion may be inserted in the root, when it is called a root graft. If inserted in the main stem about the surface of the ground, it is called a crown graft. With young trees the entire top is sometimes cut off and the scion is inserted in the main stem, just below where the top grew. This is called a stem graft. When the operation is performed on large trees, the scions are inserted in the limbs. This is top grafting. Many different modes of inserting the graft are practiced, known respectively as cleft grafting, whip grafting, veneer grafting, side grafting, etc. For the purposes for which this book is written, it will be necessary to describe only two methods.

CLEFT GRAFTING—Cleft grafting is a very simple operation. It is employed in grafting upon large limbs or stems, as in top grafting. The limb or stem is cut off squarely. A split is then made in the stub and the scion is inserted. The wound is then securely covered with grafting wax to exclude the air. For cleft grafting the scion should contain at least two buds, and usually it is cut to three buds. The lower

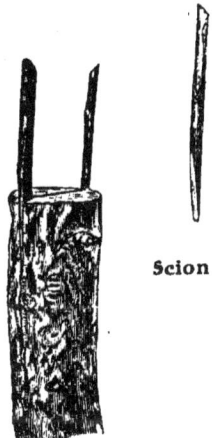

Scion

Scions Inserted

end is cut wedge-shaped to fit the cleft. The outer edge of the scion should be a little thicker than the inner. This brings the pressure on the scion where it is most required. Where the limb is large enough two scions should be inserted. This increases the chances of success. If they both grow, one may be cut off. The wound will heal over more quickly with two live scions than with one. Smooth cuts are desirable, both on the stock and scion. The main point to be observed in grafting is to have a union of the inner bark or cambis layer. These must come together in the scion and stock to give a reasonable prospect of success. For cleft-grafting the tools necessary are a fine-toothed saw to cut off the limbs. The cut may then be smoothed with a knife. A strong knife will answer to split the stub, to the depth of an inch or two. A wedge is inserted to hold the split open until the scions are inserted. Graft-

GRAFTING AND BUDDING.

ing waxes are made of beeswax, resin and tallow, or linseed oil. The proportions may be varied accordingly as hard or soft wax is wanted. One pound beeswax, four pounds resin and ½ pint of raw linseed oil make a hard wax, suitable for very warm weather. Put all together in a pot and melt. Then pour into a pail of cold water and work or pull with the hands till the wax is of the right consistency. Usually a pint of raw oil is used with this quantity of other ingredients. The wax may be worked and applied with the hand to the graft, covering all cuts. The hands should be kept greased when handling the wax. Wax may be kept warm and applied with a brush. For this purpose a double glue pot is best. The hot water in the bottom pot serves to keep the wax warm. Grafting is most successful when done in the spring, just before the buds open, and with the apple may be continued successfully until the tree is in leaf. Scions should be dormant. Cleft grafting should be done well out on the limbs of a large tree, where they do not exceed one to one and a half inches in diameter. The illustrations show a scion prepared for grafting and a stub with scions inserted, but not yet covered with wax.

WHIP GRAFTING—This is the most common form of grafting, and is the plan generally adopted in nurseries. It may be employed on small stocks to advantage, either in root, crown or stem grafting. The stock and scion are both cut diagonally with a sharp knife, making a cut surface of one to two inches. An upward cleft or cut is then made in the scion and a downward cut in the stock. The two are then united

Whip Grafting

by showing the tongue of the scion into the cleft in the stock, care being taken to have the inner bark in each meet. The illustrations herewith show a scion and stock prepared for uniting. If a good fit is made it will only be necessary to cover the cuts well with wax, applied either warm with a brush or by hand for cold wax. Soft twine that can be broken easily, such as knitting cotton, is used for winding the grafts. This insures greater safety in handling, but is not necessary where a good job has been made. The twine should be saturated with wax by dropping the balls in melted wax. Scions should be cut in the fall. They may be placed in boxes of sand and buried outdoors over winter, or kept in a cool cellar, in sand or moss. Root-stocks may also be dug in the fall and stored where they will be convenient when required for grafting. The scions should be composed of the new wood of the previous year's growth. If tender roots are used, a much longer scion may be used and this is planted so that only one bud of the scion will be above ground. In this case some of the trees may eventually come on their own roots, by sending out roots from above the union of scion and stock. A strong two-year-old root may be cut into two or more pieces and a scion inserted in each. Thin strips of muslin, dipped in melted wax, make good bandages for winding the grafts. Root grafted trees will reach a good size for planting in permanent positions in two or three years. All shoots that start from the root are kept cut off and the scion, which forms the main stem, is trained to branch at any desired height.

Various methods of grafting succeed well with the apple. Budding is more generally employed with the plum, but both root and top-grafting may be employed with the plum. Grafting the plum should be done early in the spring, when the tree is quite dormant. Late grafting is not successful with this fruit.

BUDDING—There are also several methods of budding in use, but it will be necessary to describe only the most common method, known as shield budding. Budding is successfully employed upon nearly all fruit trees and is the general means used with stone fruits. It is also employed with roses and some other ornamentals. The operation is performed in the late summer season, at a time when the bark will peel readily and buds are sufficiently developed for use. Only a single bud is used, with as little wood as possible, and is inserted under the bark. Buds of the current season's growth are used, and only well developed buds should be selected, such as will be found toward the centre of a cutting of new growth. The buds toward the tip will be too young, and those at the base not sufficiently developed. Plums will usually be in good condition for budding about the middle of August, in this climate, varying somewhat according to the season. In a dry season the wood ripens earlier and budding may be done to advantage also somewhat earlier than usual. Budding is usually done on young trees, during the second season of growth. The plants are grown from seed the first year. They are taken up in the fall and "heeled in" over winter. In the spring they are planted out and budded in the summer of the same season. Stocks one-half inch in diameter are large enough for budding. The bud is inserted as close to the ground as it can be conveniently done. It should be inserted on the north side of the stock, as a protection against drying out. A switch containing the buds is cut from a tree of the desired variety. The leaves are pinched off, leaving the stem of the leaf attached to the trunk. This serves as a handle by which to handle the buds. The buds are cut from the branch with a thin-bladed knife. Knives made specially for budding may be purchased. A very little wood and some bark is cut out with the bud, the cut being about an inch or less long. As the bark of the wood unites with the stock, the least amount of wood possible should be taken with the bud. A vertical cut through the bark, an inch or more long, is then made in the stock, with a crosscut near the top. The bark at the corners is then lifted or turned up a little and the bud is inserted and shoved down under the bark. If the bark is in the best condition and peels readily, the operation of inserting the bud is not difficult. Any portion of the bud, if any, projecting above the crosscut should be cut off. When securely inserted the stock is wrapped to hold the bud firmly in place, and prevent drying out. Careful wrapping is important. The cut should be well covered except directly over the bud. Soft cord or raffia bark are used for tying. Soft

yarn will answer. The illustrations show: (1) a bud cut out ready for inserting in the stock. (2) The stock prepared to receive the bud. (3) The bud inserted. 4. The stock properly wrapped. The leaf stem is left attached to the bud, as shown in the illustrations. As soon as the bud has united to the stock, which will be in two or three weeks, the tying material is removed. If left on too long it will cramp the stock and injure the bud. If the bud has a dry or shrivelled appearance, the work has been in vain. If it is green and fresh in appearance a good union has formed. The bud should remain dormant until the following spring. The earth should be banked up around the bud in the fall. In the spring the stock is cut off above the bud. The bud will make a rapid growth and forms the stem and top of the tree. It is not advisable to cut the entire stock off at once. A few inches may be left, and two or three weeks later it should be cut back to a half inch above the bud. All other sprouts below the bud should be kept rubbed off. It will often be necessary to tie the bud, or shoot as it has now become, to a stake to prevent breaking from wind. Wax is not used in budding.

Budding is most commonly employed on young trees, but it may also be employed for top-working on old trees. The operation is not as readily performed on old wood, and for top-working an older tree young limbs should be selected. Apple stocks may be used quite successfully for either budding or grafting. For the stone fruits budding is more successful than grafting.

CHAPTER XVI.

HANDLING AND PLANTING NURSERY STOCK.

The saying that "whatever is worth doing is worth doing well" applies with double force to the care and planting of trees and nursery stock in general. In our somewhat dry and severe climate, careful planting and good cultivation is especially desirable. Passing along a road a few years ago, the writer had his attention drawn to two men who were planting trees close by. After watching them plant two or three trees, he remarked to his companion that not ten of the trees would grow. The men were certainly doing their work expeditiously, but anything but well. Passing the place later in the season, only a very few trees appeared to be alive. Another case: A few years ago several men were observed planting trees around a public property in Winnipeg. The day was bright and warm. The first thing they did was to distribute the trees all around the property wherever they were to be planted. The trees were thrown down in the warm sun, to the number of over 100, before any other preparation for planting had been made. Nothing but failure can result from such crude work as this.

A tree out of the ground should be regarded somewhat as a fish out of water, and every care should be given it until it is properly planted again. A fish will live for some little time out of water if its gills are kept moist. A tree will likewise live for some time out of the ground if its roots are kept moist, and it is protected from sun and drying wind. Nursery stock should be unpacked as soon as received. A cool cellar is a good place for unpacking. If the stock is dry, it may be buried, root and branch, in damp earth for a time, until thoroughly moistened up, or it may even be immersed in water until completely freshened. If it is not desirable to plant at once, stock in good condition will not take any harm from being kept in a cold cellar for a few days, providing the roots are kept moist and covered with moss or litter. Strawberry plants should not be kept in a dark place. Special directions for handling these is given in the chapter on strawberries. Trees may be heeled in temporarily in a moist, shady place, after unpacking, but it is usually desirable to plant stock received in the spring as soon as possible. In heeling in, the roots should be well covered with damp earth. A good plan is to practice what is called mudding the roots before planting. A hole is dug and into this water is poured and stirred up until a mud bath is formed. The roots of the trees are then placed in the bath. For large trees, they should be planted directly from the bath, taking out one at a time as they are required and as the place for planting is made ready. The roots of small trees should not be exposed for an instant. This precaution is particularly necessary in handling evergreens. A few minutes' exposure to the sun on a bright, warm day means death to them. A cool cloudy day should be selected for planting if possible. Small trees should be carried in buckets of thin mud or water and planted directly from these. Herbaceous plants may be carried in boxes, with a layer of damp moss over them.

PREPARING TO PLANT—The general principles of planting are much the same, whether the thing to be planted is a strawberry plant or a tree of considerable size. The first thing is to prepare the object

HANDLING STOCK.

in hand for planting. All broken or bruised roots should be cut off, making a slanting cut from the under side upward, so the cut surface will rest naturally upon the soil. Long, heavy roots should be shortened up. A long, thick root is of little advantage, and is better cut off than planted in a cramped position. New roots will start out from the place where the old root is cut off, and it does not matter much whether these new roots start one foot or two feet from the tree. The top should be cut back in proportion at least to the roots. This is very important, if vigorous, healthy trees are desired. A tree that has been dug up and lost considerable of its roots cannot be expected to support the entire top. It must be given every opportunity to overcome the shock it has received from being torn from the soil. The tree should be pruned out before planting and the growth of the previous year should be cut back about one-half. All trees, shrubs, bush fruits, etc., should be treated the same way. The illustration herewith shows a tree marked for cutting back before planting. If trees should be received in a frozen state,

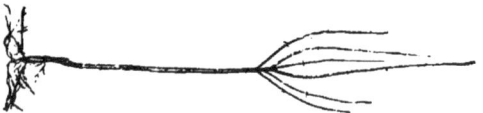

they should be buried until they thaw, or they may be left in a cold cellar to thaw slowly, before unpacking. Freezing will not injure hardy stock provided they are not thawed out by exposure to the air. The fibrous roots of herbaceous plants like strawberries may be shortened back before planting, and some of the foliage may be removed. If flower buds are showing, pinch them off.

HOW TO PLANT—Dig holes considerably larger than the roots, so the roots can be placed in their natural position and without cramping. Throw the top earth on one side, and the subsoil on the other, when digging the hole, and use the mellow, top earth about the roots. Sift in the fine earth about the roots and be sure that the soil is thoroughly packed around the roots. This rule should be observed in planting practically everything, from a tree to a small bedding plant. In heavy soil, when damp, it will not require so much pressure to properly firm the soil, but in light or dry soil, all the pressure that can be exerted with the foot is necessary. No air spaces should be left among the roots. With large trees the packing must be done while gradually filling in the earth. The packing should be done among and around the roots, but not on the surface. After the roots are well covered and packed, fill in with loose earth. Do not bank up around trees. It is better to leave a depression around the tree. If the soil is dry when planting, water thoroughly before filling in with loose earth, leaving the dry, loose earth on the surface. Watering trees is usually not necessary in an ordinary season, but in a very dry year it will be necessary to water newly planted trees. This should be done by removing the loose surface earth and giving the tree a thorough watering, then fill in the loose, dry earth again. This prevents the baking of the surface, which should always be loose. The custom of frequently sprinkling or watering lightly is injurious. It bakes the soil and causes "damping off" in young seedlings. Water thoroughly, if it is required, and then abstain from further applications until it is really needed. Shrubs or avenue trees are frequently planted in sod. When this is necessary, extra care should be taken in planting. A much larger and deeper hole should be dug and the tree or shrub should be planted in good earth from the garden. The sod should be removed for a distance of three feet all around the tree, and this space should be kept cultivated, by spading up in the spring and shallower cultivation thereafter. Sod around the trees robs them of moisture. The cultivated space should be kept as level as possible, and not rounded up so as to slope away from the tree. As a general rule trees should be planted considerably deeper than they grew in the nursery, but much depends on the character of the soil and the size of the tree. In very heavy, damp soil, it may not be advisable to plant more than a couple of inches deeper than the tree grew, while in very dry locations, where the soil is loose and porous, up to a foot deeper is not too much for a three-year-old tree. Too deep planting on heavy soil will be indicated by a late, slow growth, and sometimes a tendency of the leaves to curl. Trees planted deep in cold soil in April or May have been known to stand until July, or even later, before making new growth. Trees have been known to remain dormant until the following spring, one year from the time of planting. In such cases the top usually dies, and a new growth starts from the root or stem. Trees making a late growth will usually winter kill. Manure should not be used about the roots of trees. If manure is used, spread it over the surface as a mulch. A good mulch in the fall is always advisable, as a protection to the roots, for retaining moisture, etc. Mulch also keeps the ground cool and moist in summer, but frequent surface cultivation is better. Do not mulch in the spring while the ground is frozen. The theory that mulching on top of the frozen ground in the spring will hold trees back is a fallacy, and the practice is liable to do serious injury to the trees, by keeping their roots encased in frost, while the tops are exposed to a warm temperature. Frost at the roots will not keep fruit trees from blossoming. In planting large trees in hard soil setting off a charge of dynamite in the hole will loosen up the earth and reduce the necessary labor.

PRUNING—For fruit trees, very little pruning will be required beyond the pruning given at the time of planting. In our climate a thick head should be encouraged. Pruning is best done when the sprouts are quite young and soft. Small sprouts may be rubbed or cut off at any time, regardless of the time of year. If proper attention is given to the growth and training of the tree, it will seldom be necessary to remove large limbs. With fruit trees about the only pruning necessary is to remove branches that rub or interfere with other parts of the tree. This should be done, as stated, when the shoots are small. With evergreens very little pruning can be done at any time, hence the necessity for extra care in planting. It would spoil the appearance of an evergreen to cut it back. The root is therefore obliged to carry the strain of practically the full top. With ornamental trees and shrubs, it is well to know the nature of each species or variety, in order to prune intelligently. The hydangea, for instance, like most roses, produces it superb bloom upon the new growth of the current season, hence severe cutting back in the spring improves the bloom. The lilac, on the other hand, produces its flowers from the terminal buds formed the previous year. To cut back the lilac would destroy the bloom. Pruning should be done intelligently and with a definite object in view. Otherwise better not prune at all. The man who has gained his experience of pruning in a moist, mild climate, should not be turned loose among trees here with pruning utensils. Branches that are causing the tree to overgrow in any direction may be checked by cutting back. For shade, lawn, and most other trees, a main, central stem is the best form. Branches that are growing too strongly, and showing a tendency to overshadow the main stem may be checked by cutting back. Branches should start alternately one above the other. Two opposite branches from one stem make weak crotches, which are liable to break or split, and destroy the appearance of the tree. Splits may be drawn together by using iron bolts. Sometimes the damage caused in this way will be entirely overcome in time, by a uniting and overgrowing of the split. The best time to prune is a disputed point. Pruning when a tree is dormant forces new growth. Pruning when the tree is in leaf checks growth, by removing a portion of the leaf surface, thus checking the food supply of the tree, for the leaves are both the stomach and lungs of a plant. Many trees, like the maple, will bleed severely if pruned in the spring. Pruning done in the early summer will heal over quickly. Light pruning, as stated, may safely be done any time. Heavy pruning will rarely be necessary where trees or plants have received proper care. If limbs of some size have to be removed, early summer is perhaps the best time, as they will then heal rapidly. All limbs or shoots should be cut close to the main stem, so as not to leave a stub to decay. A clean, smooth cut, close to the stem or main branch, will heal over, while a stub will not. All wounds of any size should be covered with grafting wax or thick paint.

TIME TO PLANT—Generally speaking, the early spring is the safest time to plant most things in our climate. This applies to practically all large trees. Some of the small fruits may be safely planted in the fall, for which directions are given in the chapter on currants. Some of the hardy shrubs and trees of small size may be safely planted in the fall, providing the soil is in good condition and is sufficiently moist. In a very dry season fall planting would not be desirable. The same directions as for spring planting should be followed, and in addition the plants should be banked up well with earth, or by bending the tops over and covering entirely with earth. If properly planted and covered, many plants will do better than if left until spring. The plants become well established and are ready to start at once in the spring. If the following summer is dry and unfavorable, the fall planting has a decided advantage. Many of the hardy herbaceous plants, such as the paeony, hardy lillies, etc., succeed better from fall planting, when the soil is in good condition. Fairly early fall planting, to enable the plants to become established before winter, is best. In our climate this would be toward the end of September or early in October.

HEELING IN TREES—The term "heeling in" is applied to storing or burying trees over winter for planting in the spring. There are many advantages in favor of this practice, compared with digging and shipping trees in the spring. Where shipment is made long distances the advantage of fall shipment is even greater. The weather in the fall is generally cooler and more favorable for the digging and handling of trees. For long distance shipments they can be handled in better condition. Trees and other plants are in a more thoroughly dormant condition in the fall. There is a little rhyme the children sing, which reads:

> Mid the snowing and the blowing and the cruel sleet,
> Little flowers begin their growing, far beneath our feet.

This is quite true. Plants start into life while their roots are still encased in frost. Poplars and willows may be seen in bloom with banks of snow at their base. Before the plants can be dug in the spring they are fully awake and have started the new season's growth. In the case of long distance shipments, they are often out in leaf before their destination is reached. Our spring season, is short and frequently sets in very warm, early and suddenly. Such weather is unfavorable for handling nursery stock. Stock secured in the fall is at hand when the best time for planting comes around. Another important point is the callusing of the roots. Where trees are received in the fall the roots should be trimmed at once as for planting in the spring. When a root is cut a callus forms over the cut surface and new roots start from this callus. This callus always forms first. When the trimming is done in the fall the callus is formed and the tree is ready to make new roots by the time planting is done in the spring. Trees dug in the fall and properly stored over winter will usually make a healthier and stronger growth than stock dug in the spring. Of course a great deal depends on the manner in which the stock has been stored over winter. There is no better way to keep stock than by heeling in, if the work is carefully performed. For heeling in nursery stock, a high and dry spot in cultivated ground should be selected. A trench is then dug, having one side sloping to the top. In this the trees are spread out, with the roots in the bottom of the trench, and the tops resting upon or inclined toward the level ground. The soil should be worked in well among the roots as in planting, and firmed with the foot, and the trench filled up. The tops should rest on the surface of the ground and be entirely covered with six inches to a foot of earth. Bank up the earth over the roots, so as to have them covered deeply. Complete covering with earth will generally keep out mice. A covering of manure or other mulch may be added later, but this should not be put on until fairly cold weather sets in, as it is not advisable to have the trees too warm. Stock stored in this way will come out in fine condition in the spring, and generally thrive better than trees that have been dug in the spring. All kinds of deciduous trees and shrubs may be handled in this way. Many herbaceous plants may also be buried in the soil or in sand with perfect safety. Evergreens and strawberry plants should not be stored in this way.

WHAT TO PLANT—This will depend upon the tastes of the individual. Whether it be fruits or ornamental trees the same general rules apply as to the selection of stock. Most people make the mistake of trying to secure large plants. A good root is of more importance than a large top. A compact, fibrous root is better than a large thick root. In moist, mild climates larger trees may be handled with greater safety than here. In our climate best results will be attained by planting young trees. The best age for planting most trees and shrubs is two years, and it must be remembered that trees at two years, grown here, are not nearly as large as trees of the same age grown farther south. An apple tree, for instance, grown here will usually range from three to four feet when two years old. Farther south trees of six feet at two years are common. If large trees are supplied the purchaser will be fairly safe in concluding that the trees have been brought in from the south. Even in our short seasons, however, the growth of vigorous stock is frequently surprising. Frequently nothing is gained by planting large trees. Healthy, young trees will often outgrow much larger ones in the course of two or three years, and make stronger and handsomer trees. The reason for this is easily explained. Large trees have to be cut back so severely in order to give them a fair chance for life, that their form is often seriously injured, and an unsightly tree is the result. If they are not cut back they will likely remain puny and delicate or die. It is a severe shock to the tree to dig it up and move it to a new location. It suffers in the loss of roots and from being out of it natural element for a time. The loss of roots to the small tree is proportionately not as great, and the shock of removal not nearly as severely felt. The small tree will recover much more quickly, and will frequently make a larger and better tree in a few years than trees of double or treble the size at the time of planting. Those who are in a hurry to secure large trees often defeat the very object they have in view by planting large specimens. At the same time quite large trees may sometimes be successfully handled, where it is necessary to move them only short distances. In this case they should be handled with a large clump of earth upon the roots.

When trees are required in large numbers for shelter belts, wind breaks, or forest plantations, it is best to secure plants one year old. They are not nearly as expensive and require very much less labor in planting.

CHAPTER XVII.

THE HOME GARDEN AND SURROUNDINGS.

It is not the intention in this chapter to undertake to give instructions for improving and beautifying the surroundings of the home on a pretentious scale. Where this work is to be undertaken on an extensive scale best results will be attained by securing the services of a practical landscape gardener, whose experienced eye will readily take in the situation and enable him to make such plans as will be best adapted to the individual requirements of different situations. Instructions cannot be given in writing to cover all cases, as each location will have peculiarities of its own which would necessitate more or less change from any general rules which may be given. Much can be said, however, which will assist those who wish to improve the surroundings of the home, and particularly the farm or suburban home. About the new homes of the settlers in these provinces, it is not expected that we will find as good gardens and as pleasant surroundings as in the older established homes of countries which have been much longer settled. In some cases some attempt has been made at planting trees and establishing a garden, but it is the exception rather than the rule in the country districts. More might be done, and more should be done to improve the surroundings of the rural home. From an economic point of view, it is profitable to

Lawn Scenes in Grounds of Buchanan Nurseries
St. Charles, Manitoba

give attention to these matters. Every tree planted and cared for on the prairie home adds value to the property. There is, perhaps, no way by which a farm property can be increased in value at less cost, than by improving and beautifying the place by the planting of trees and shrubs and other similar improvements. But the value added to the property is of much less importance than the comfort that may be obtained from pleasant surroundings. The influence of such surroundings is inspiring and refining. The children brought up under such influences will have a kindlier regard for "the old home" and will think of it with feelings of pleasure in after life. All these things are worth trying for,

THE HOME GARDEN.

and the man who has the best interests of his family at heart, will try to do what he can to make their home as homelike and pleasant as possible.

Then there is the vegetable and fruit garden, without which life in the country cannot be at all what it should be, either from the standpoint of comfort or health. On many of our farms a miserable diet of pork, bread and tea is the regular thing. The most healthful foods which the earth produces are the products of the garden, yet these are lacking, or at best meagerly supplied in many a country home, while right at the door they could be produced in variety and abundance. In spite of our short seasons, which necessitate unusual activity during the summer season, scarcity of help, and the many things which have to be undertaken in the new homes of this country, some attention should be given to the vegetable and fruit garden, and to the improvement of the home by planting trees and shrubs.

The labor necessary to maintain a good garden may be greatly reduced by a little systematic planning. It can be so laid out that nearly all the work of cultivating can be done with the horse. A man, a horse and a cultivator will do more work in a properly laid out garden in a couple of hours, than would be done by several persons in days. The cultivator will also do far better work than is done by hand implements. About many farms and rural homes little patchy gardens are seen, worked up by hand. Vegetables planted in raised beds, often in front of the house. The approach to the front of the house is sometimes between rows of currant bushes. This plan entails unnecessary labor and is an eye-sore to a person of refined tastes. The fruit and vegetable garden should not be in front of the house. There should be an easy approach to the front of the house, through as pleasant surroundings as possible. Where there is plenty of land and room, provision should ue made for an open lawn of considerable size in front of the house. Trees are better planted at some little distance from the house. Trees and shrubs should not be planted in single specimens, but should be grown in clumps, with the lower growing varieties in front of the taller kinds. Clumps may be massed at some distance to the side of the house, and particularly in locations where they will cut off or hide undesirable views. The view of the barnyard may be shut off by a hedge or screen of trees. A pleasant view in any direction should not be interrupted by trees. Planting trees too close to the buildings is a frequent error, which is in keeping with the common mistake of locating the house too close to the road. The farmhouse should be a few hundred feet from the road.

The vegetable and fruit garden should be convenient to the house, so that occasional spare moments between other work may be devoted to the garden. Something to do may always be found in the garden. All planting should be done in rows, the full length of the garden plot, whether it be vegetables or fruit, and level cultivation is usually the best. Avoid small plots or planting in beds as requiring unnecessary labor. In this way most of the work of cultivating may be done with the one-horse cultivator, while spaces between narrow rows of vegetables may be cultivated with the wheel hoe. With the latter instrument five or six times as much work can be done as with the ordinary hand hoe. Vegetables may be grown between the rows of fruit trees or bushes, for the

THE HOME GARDEN.

first year or two after planting, until the space is required by the plants. It is better to give plenty of space than to crowd the rows. When plants are first put out they will appear to have plenty of room, but when they grow large and spread toward each other it will often be found that they are crowded, causing inconvenience in cultivating and gathering the crop. The farm or rural garden should contain an abundance of all the common vegetables and fruits, so as to provide the table liberally in quantity and variety during the summer, and ensure an ample store for winter. A liberal space should be allowed for those two valuable early spring appetizers—rhubarb and asparagus. The latter, so seldom seen in the farm garden, is as easily grown as potatoes. By attention to the garden, the health and happiness of the family will be greatly increased

THE WIND-BREAK—The wind-break, or shelter belt, should be an early consideration at every farm home. Any one who has lived for

Windbreak of Hardy Willows, 9 Feet High, 15 Months After Cuttings were Planted.

one winter on the open prairie, after experiencing the advantages afforded by the shelter of timber, will not need any argument to convince him of the value of the shelter-belt. It is an economy and a comfort which no progressive farmer can afford to be without. The shelter belts should be established on a comprehensive scale, so as to enclose the farm buildings and garden and afford ample room within their protecting influences. Many wind-breaks have been planted too close to buildings, causing the formation of banks of snow where they are a great inconvenience. This can be avoided by planting the proper distance from buildings. A row of trees planted 50 to 100 feet outside of the main shelter-belt will cause the snow to bank in the vacant space between the breaks, thus preventing the snow from banking in among the trees and breaking them down. The protection of wind-breaks is necessary where a good garden is desired, especially if fruits are to be grown. With such protection at least some species and varieties of fruit may be grown in the most severe locations, while without protection the best results cannot be attained in the most favored localities. The clumps of ornamental trees and shrubs about the house, which are referred to earlier in this chapter, would of course come within the lines of the wind-breaks. Such clumps of trees or shrubs planted or massed irregularly along the inner rows of the shelter-belt, would tend to soften the otherwise rigid appearance of the long, straight rows of trees. Fruit trees should not be planted so close to the wind-break that they will be robbed of moisture, nor in a position where the snow will bank over them and break the limbs. Strawberries, small fruits and herbaceous plants may be grown to advantage where the snow will cover them deeply.

The land for the wind-break should be carefully prepared the previous year and plowed deeply. It should be in a good state of cultivation and, if new land, the sod should be thoroughly worked out. Small trees of one season's growth are best for planting of this kind. They may be quickly planted by plowing deep furrows. The plow should be run at least twice through each furrow, up and back. A line is then stretched along the furrow and the planting proceeds. Plant small trees two inches deeper than they grew in the nursery, and get the root down straight. Don't cramp the roots. On light soil plant even deeper. A dibber or pointed stick may be used to make a hole for the tap root of small trees, where the furrow is not deep enough, but a narrow spade does better work.

There are many varieties of trees well adapted to planting for shelter-belts and wind-breaks. Some of the best are the Manitoba maple, native elm and ash, Russian willow and native spruce. The golden and sharp-leaved willows are especially valuable where a quick growth is desired. They will attain a height of seven to ten feet in two years with good cultivation. Cultivation is best accomplished by running the one-horse cultivator between the rows. This should be started soon after planting and thereafter every ten days or two weeks during the growing season. Keep up cultivation each year until the trees cover the space so closely that further work of this nature cannot be done. The main object in frequent cultivation is to conserve moisture, and encourage rapid growth, and keep the ground free from grass and weeds. The absence of weeds should not lead to any lessening of cultivation, which must be kept up whether weeds are present or not, to ensure good results. The distance apart to plant trees is a disputed point. Some of the best authorities say the rows should be six to ten feet apart. Others say three to four feet. There are good arguments in favor of both wide and close planting. Where wide planting is done, the trees will branch out from the ground, making a thick cover from the ground upward. In close planting the lower limbs will die back and a straight upward growth is encouraged. The more vigorous trees will crowd out or overgrow the weaker ones. If timber is wanted, close planting is advisable. About four feet apart each way is advised for most trees. As close as three feet is advised by some authorities. In close planting the trees will quickly shade the ground and cultivation will have to cease much sooner, but it is doubtful if an early stoppage of cultivation is an advantage in the long run. Where only three or four rows are planted it is desirable to plant, say six feet, and continue cultivation until strong, vigorous, bushy trees are obtained. For a wood lot or wide break the closer plan of planting is desirable. Russian poplars and cottonwood require more room than the varieties mentioned earlier in this chapter, as they do not stand crowding. These varieties make a strong, quick growth, but the cottonwood is a rather thin tree where shade is desired. It is a good plan to mix varieties in the shelter belt or forest plantation. Where only a few rows are planted, the middle rows should be composed of compact, bushy trees, such as the Russian willows. Outside of these Manitoba maple, ash, elm and Russian poplar. The varieties may be varied to suit the nature of the soil. Cottonwood thrives best on moist land. The Manitoba maple will do on either medium light or heavy soil. On dry, light soil the Russian poplar and acutifolia willow are valuable; also the native white spruce. Ash and elm thrive on clay, or loam soils, but not on dry, sandy soils. The number of trees required for planting a given space may easily be ascertained when the length and number of rows and distance apart in the rows is decided upon. No pruning should be done in the shelter belt.

CHAPTER XVIII.

PLANT DISEASES, INJURIOUS INSECTS, SPRAYING MIXTURES.

An enormous loss is annually occasioned through the depredations of various plant insects. Almost every plant that grows is subject to the attacks of insects. Each plant has its insects which may be said to be peculiarly its own. But the destruction to plant life is not confined to insects alone. Fungous diseases are also common to nearly all plants. The parasitic fungi are weeds which grow upon the leaves, stems or fruit of plants. Not having the power of obtaining nourishment from the soil, they fasten themselves upon more highly organized plants and drain from these the already prepared plant food. They are reproduced by spores, which are thrown off in great numbers and carried by wind or insects to other plants. The delicate threads of the fungi penetrate the plant and absorb the nourishment which should go to build up the plant and produce fruit.

Good cultivation is a material aid in holding plant diseases in check. A system of spraying has also come into wide use, with the object of overcoming both fungous diseases and troublesome insects. Fortunately spraying mixtures may be prepared which comprise remedies for both insects and fungi in one treatment. A great variety of spraying machinery and appliances are now obtainable, from a hand syringe costing a dollar up to power machines costing hundreds of dollars. In the fruit regions spraying is now systematically practiced. In fact in some sections of the south and east some crops would be unprofitable if spraying were not resorted to. The potato is an example of a plant which in some parts gives very poor returns unless systematically sprayed, owing to the prevalence of blight. This potato disease has been quite common in sections of Manitoba in some recent years, and if it should continue to spread, spraying may have to be resorted to here more generally than it has in the past.

The commodity most commonly used in preparing mixtures for all fungi is copper sulphate (blue-stone). Every farmer in the West knows the value of this as a germicide to destroy smut spores in grain. For spraying upon plants the blue-stone is dissolved in water and combined with lime. The lime is used to neutralize the caustic properties of the blue-stone and prevent burning of the foliage. Paris green is combined with the preparation to destroy leaf-eating insects. There is a numerous class of insects known as sucking insects. These do not eat the foliage and consequently they cannot be readily poisoned. They suck the juices of the plant from beneath the surface, and are consequently quite as injurious as some of the leaf-eaters. The sucking insects are more difficult to treat. The object in spraying preparations in dealing with this class of insects is to use something that will kill them by contact. Coal oil is death to most insects, and this is the basis of such spraying mixtures. Soap is used to form an emulsion, so that the oil can be evenly mixed with water.

The greatest benefit will be derived from spraying by giving early treatment, either for insects or fungi, but particularly for the latter. If any form of fungous disease is feared, spraying should be done before the trouble appears. For trees and shrubs a strong solution is valuable before the buds break in the spring. This is valuable for black-knot, plum-pocket, and other forms of fungi. The ordinary fungicide, prepared with lime and blue-stone, is known as Bordeaux mixture. This may be used double strength before the buds open. Other applications are usually given just before the blossoms open, or soon after they fall, with the ordinary strength Bordeaux mixture, and later in the season as occasion may demand. A machine that will throw a fine, mist-like spray with considerable force, is better than one that gives a coarse, drenching spray. The formulae are as follows:

BORDEAUX MIXTURE.

Copper Sulphate (blue-stone) 4 lbs.
Lime (fresh), 4 lbs.
Water, 40 gallons.
Add 4 oz. of Paris green when leaf-eating insects are present.

This is prepared as follows: Half fill a barrel with water. Put the blue-stone in a bag and suspend it in the water. It will dissolve in a short time, while if thrown loose into the barrel it will not dissolve readily. In another vessel slake the lime, using four or five gallons of water. When the blue-stone is dissolved and the lime thoroughly slaked, strain the latter into the barrel containing the blue-stone. The straining is to keep out any gritty matter which may clog the sprayer. Very small particles in the solution will interfere with the work. Clean vessels should, therefore, be used. The barrel may then be filled up with water, stirred, and the mixture is ready for use. This is the standard mixture for all kinds of blight, rust or other fungi. If this is found too strong for some plants with tender foliage, it may be reduced by adding water,

PLANT DISEASES.

but most plants will stand this strength. It is frequently used stronger, or with up to 6 lbs. of blue-stone to the barrel. For potato blight the 6-lb. strength is used. More Paris Green may also be used for potatoes. For leaf-eating insects alone, Paris green is used in the strength of about four to six ounces to the barrel of water. Lime should be used with Paris green in the proportion of double the amount of Paris green used. It is generally better to use the Paris green in Bordeaux mixture.

KEROSENE EMULSION.

Kerosene (coal oil), 2 gallons.
Rain water, 1 gallon.
Soap, ½ lb.

Boil the soap in the water till dissolved. Pour it into the kerosene while boiling and churn vigorously with a force pump (a sprayng machine will answer) for a few minutes. If the emulsion is right it will thicken when cool to the consistency of thin jelly. This will keep for a considerable time. Dilute this emulsion in eight to ten gallons of water, for use. Spraying with a solution made from steeping tobacco stems in water is very useful for plant lice. Gardeners can grow the tobacco for this purpose. This sometimes gives better results than the kerosene emulsion. Use two pounds of tobacco refuse to five gallons of water.

BRAN MASH FOR CUT WORMS.

Bran, 25 pounds.
Paris green, ½ pound.

Sweeten with molasses and add enough water to moisten the mass slightly. Scatter or drop this among the plants. This is the most effective remedy for cut-worms. They eat it in preference to the plants.

HELLEBORE FOR LEAF EATERS.

White Hellebore, 1 ounce.
Water, 2 gallons.

Useful for currant worm. Not so poisonous as Paris green and does not stain the fruit.

GOOSEBERRY MILDEW.

One ounce of Liver of sulphur dissolved in two gallons of hot water. Spray early and often.

WASH FOR TREE BORERS.

Make a strong solution of washing soda. Add soft soap to make a thick paint. Paint the trunk and large limbs. A ½ pint of crude carbolic acid may be added.

FOR POTATO SCAB.

Soak the seed potatoes for two hours in a solution made of ½ pint of formalin to 15 gallons of water.

PYRETHRUM POWDER.

Pyrethrum powder may be mixed with five times the quantity of flour and dusted upon plants. Useful for squash and cucumber bugs and cabbage worms.

WHALE OIL SOAP.

One pound dissolved in seven gallons of hot water. Useful for plant lice. Sponging the leaves of house plants with ordinary soap suds is useful for plant lice.

CHAPTER XIX.

TREES, SHRUBS AND PLANTS RECOMMENDED FOR THE PRAIRIE PROVINCES.

The following list of trees, shrubs and plants is recommended for planting throughout the prairie provinces, with some limitations as to locality and nature of soil. It is to be understood that these species and varieties are recommended only where northern grown stock is secured. While trees grown here will generally prove hardy, the same species or varieties, if brought in from the east or south, or grown here from eastern or southern seed, will often turn out quite useless.

TREES FOR SHELTER BELTS OR FOREST PLANTATIONS.

Acer negundo—(Manitoba Maple).
Betula papyrifera—(Native Birch).
Fraxinus pennsylvanica—(Native green ash).
Larix laricina—(Native larch or tamarac).
Populus balsamifera—(Balsam poplar or Balm of Gilead).
Populus deltoides—(Cottonwood). Best adapted to deep, moist land.
Russian poplars—Several forms. For light soil.
Salix—(Willow). The best are Russian golden willow, acute-leaved willow, Russian laurel willow, white willow.
Tilia americana—(Native basswood).—Eastern Manitoba only.
Ulmus americana—(Native elm).

EVERGREEN TREES.

Abies balsamea—(Balsam spruce or fir).
Picea—(Spruce)—The native white spruce (picea alba) thrives on light soil. The native black spruce (picea nigra) on moist soil.
Picea pungens—(Colorado spruce).
Pinus divaricata or pinus banksiana—(Jack pine).
Pinus sylvestris, Pinus sylvestris rigaensis—(Scotch pine). The latter is rather the hardier form.

Most of the trees in these lists are suitable also for street or avenue

HARDY PLANTS.

purposes, or for ornamental planting. All the evergreens are ornamental. The laurel and golden willows and tamarac are good ornamental trees. The elm and Manitoba maple have been most largely planted for street trees. Basswood is also a good street tree where it can be grown to advantage, but it does not thrive west of the Red river valley, or at least on the higher altitudes west. Ash, elm, cottonwood, willows and tamarac will grow on heavy and moist land. Russian poplars, white spruce and pine thrive on light soil. Black spruce will grow on heavier and damper soil than the white, but is not as valuable a tree.

ORNAMENTAL TREES AND SHRUBS.

Acer tataricum ginnala—(Asiatic maple).
Artemisia—Old man, southerwood).
Berberis—(Barberry)—Common barberry, purple leaved barberry, Thunberg's barberry.
Betula alba laciniata—(Cut leaved birch).
Caragana—Several forms.
Cornus—(Dogwood)—Native red and Siberian forms.
Cotoneaster acutifolia—(Sharp leaved cotoneaster).
Crataegus coccinea—(Scarlet thorn).
Eleagnus angustifolia—(Russian olive).
Lonicera tatarica—(Bush honeysuckles)—Several forms.
Prunus Pennsylvanica.—Bird cherry).
Prunus nigra—(Manitoba plum).
Prunus pumila—(Sand or bush cherry).
Pyrus baccata—(Wild Russian or Siberian crab).
Pyrus americana—(Native mountain ash).
Ribes alpinum—(Mountain Currant).
Rhus glabra—(Native Sumach).
Rosa rugosa—(Rugosa rose).
Shepherdia argentea—Buffalo berry).
Syringa—(Lilacs)—Common purple and white, and varieties thereof, Josikae lilac, villosa lilac, Persia lilac.
Spirea salicifolia—(Meadow sweet).
Viburnum—Viburnum lantana, viburnum opulus (high bush cranberry), viburnum lantana (sheep berry).

VINES AND CLIMBERS.

Ampelopsis quinquefolia—(Virginia creeper).—Native form.
Celastrus scandeus—(Bitter sweet).—Native form.
Vitis riparia—(Manitoba wild or frost grape).

There are many shrubs that could be added to those given, which may be grown in specially favored locations, or where they have special care. Some are left out which are fairly hardy, but not entirely robust in all situations. Others rarely give favorable results. Some of those omitted are: European mountain ash, which is hardy in some locations. Spiraea van houttei, which is fairly hardy in many locations, as are also Spiraea sorbifolia, Spiraea opulifolia, or ninebark, Spiraea revesii, etc. The common snowball, or guelder rose, gives fair results in favored locations. Several of the buckthorns are hardy and are useful for hedges or ornamental shrubs. The golden and common elders usually kill back somewhat, but this does not seem to injure the plants, which make a strong growth from the roots. The Philadelphus, or mock oranges, is sometimes recommended, but it should be tried only in the most favored locations. Hydrange paniculatu grandiflora is a fine shrub which may be grown in favored locations or with good winter protection. Requires moist situation and will stand severe cutting back in the spring.

SHRUBS FOR HEDGES.

Some of the best hardy shrubs for screens and hedges are: buckthorn, caragana, buffalo-berry, common lilac, bush honeysuckle, Artemesia, Pyrus baccata, barberry. The last named for favored locations.

HERBACEOUS PERENNIAL FLOWERS.

Herbaceous perennials are those plants which die down on the approach of winter and grow up again from the roots in the spring. A large number of the perennial flowers are hardy here, including many of the very finest species and varieties. In our short seasons the perennials are specially desirable. By a judicious selection of varieties, an abundance of bloom may be had from early spring until the close of the season. An herbaceous flower border will add greatly to the attractiveness of the home and prove a source of pleasure throughout the season. The perennials require rather less labor than the annuals and when established are surer bloomers. The following is a list of some of the best: Achillea ptarmica (the pearl), Aquilegia (columbine), Campanula (Canterbury Bell), Delphinium (larkspur) in variety, Dicentra spectabilis (bleeding heart), Gaillardia, Iris (German), Lilium tigrnum (tiger lilly), very hardy; Hemerocallis flava (lemon lilly), Paeonia (peony), magnificent flowers. The rose of the herbaceous border. Papaver orientalis (oriental poppy), Papaver nudicule, (Icelandic poppy), Phlox (perennial phlox), one of the best; Rudbeckia (golden glow), a fine late bloomer; Hesperis (sweet rocket).

89047185855

b89047185855a

ook may be kept

FOURTEEN DAYS

last date stamped below. A fine of TWO CENTS
be charged for each day the book is kept over

www.ingramcontent.com/pod-product-compliance
Lightning Source LLC
LaVergne TN
LVHW011100100525
810918LV00003B/164